AMERICAN LITERATURE

A Study and Research Guide

AMERICAN LITERATURE

A Study and Research Guide

Lewis Leary
with the collaboration of
John Auchard

M. Thomas Inge, General Editor

ST. MARTIN'S PRESS / NEW YORK

To my students,
who have taught me.

Preface

This guide attempts to chart a way through the maze of writings on American literature, most of which have appeared during the past forty years, and to point toward those earlier writings that are still useful. It lists books and essays that have been of most value to the compiler; another person might suggest other sources of instruction or have other things to say about the materials that are here recommended. The study of American literature is a rich field, variously cultivated, which has yielded important harvests of many kinds. But the last word has not been spoken, for it is a living literature. As Henry David Thoreau said at the close of *Walden,*

"There is more day to dawn. The sun [that is, what greets us today, of knowledge or perception] is but a morning star."

It is hoped that this guide can do more than chart a way through what has been said and done. For there is much more to do before our cultural heritage can be understood completely and assimilated into our present view of the world and of ourselves. If what is said in the pages that follow does not act as a catalyst to produce further study and opinion, it will have been, in John Milton's term, a blind guide indeed.

The study of American literature is, finally, not the study of what has been said about American literature, but the reading of the books, poems, and essays that make up that literature. Read the best books first, counseled Thoreau. Nothing that can be said about literature is a substitute for the literature itself. This book, then, is only a guide to other guides, to what some other people have said about writing in America. That writing awaits further reading, keener interpretation, new estimates of whether it is, or is not, after all, something to be cherished or admired. And, most important, why it is, or should be, admired. Just as every generation must write its own books, so every generation must sit in judgment, not only on those books, but on books of the past that have made them possible. For books are built upon books, and there is a continuum in literary history.

Someone has said that the cornerstone of true scholarship, which in literature is appreciation at its alert and well-honed best, is informed humility—knowing what you know, respecting your own judgment, but being willing also to respect the judgments of others. As you follow leads that this guide suggests, you may discover that what has been said in evaluation of a book, an essay, or a writer is in your judgment wrong. So build your own estimate. Only in that way will the study of American literature remain fresh and lively. What is worse than drinking from a stagnant pool?

Each book recommended in this guide is identified by its place of publication, publisher, date of publication, and, in square brackets, its classification according to the Library of Congress system of classification, which is currently used by most libraries and indicates the place on the library shelves where the book can be found. One caution: some libraries find it necessary or convenient to modify the Library of Congress classification system, especially in its final digits. Therefore, consult your library card catalogue. It will not only tell you where the book is to be found in your library, but it can also lead to the discovery of other books that may prove useful. Books that are currently available in paperback editions are identified in this guide with an asterisk [*] following the title. It is presumed that most of the periodicals mentioned will be found in the periodical room of your library.

Although the compiler takes complete responsibility for the judgments expressed in the pages that follow, he has had generous assistance from several colleagues, especially Richard Harter Fogle, C. Hugh Holman, Blyden Jackson, Kimball King, and George Lensing. The presence, inspiration, and admonitions of William Harmon, Karin Gleiter, and Louis D. Rubin, Jr., have, as always, been of inestimable value. Nor could this book have been put together without the active assistance of John Auchard, the encouragement and counsel of M. Thomas Inge, and the corrective prescriptions of Nancy Barton and Toni Blood, each of whom has been a benevolent but severe taskmaster.

Finally, this book is for you, the person who uses it. It has been made in grateful recollection of thousands of students who have argued with me over the past forty years, as I hope you will argue with me now.

Lewis Leary
Chapel Hill, North Carolina

Contents

CHAPTER ELEVEN

AMERICAN LITERATURE

A Study and Research Guide

CHAPTER ONE

History of the Study and Teaching of American Literature

❦ ❦ ❦ The first signs of interest in American literature in American colleges came from the students themselves, who in the 1770s, as ties with Great Britain weakened, urged native writers to write of native scenes. They called for a new Homer, a new Milton, a new Pope to arise and sing the glories of the New World. During the American Revolution many of these young people wrote with fervent patriotism, in verse and in prose. As the war ended, literary independence seemed to many of them as important as political independence. Resenting the influence of England on native letters, one of them exploded in 1786: "Shall we ever be thought to have learning or grace, Unless it be brought from that damnable place?"

In 1793 a twenty-three-year-old named Elihu Hubbard Smith put together a volume simply called *American Poems* as the first anthology of native verse. But the study and discussion of American literature remained for many years an extracurricular activity. Classroom time was devoted to the study of Latin, Greek, and sometimes Hebrew literature. The study of any literature in English was not considered worthy of serious academic consideration. No person of culture was thought to need instruction in interpretation of any modern literature.

Sydney Smith posed a prickly question in the *Edinburgh Review* of January 1820: "In the four quarters of the globe, who reads an American book?" Several responsive statements appeared during the following decade. In 1823 Charles J. Ingersoll delivered "A Discourse Concerning the Influence of America on the Mind" before the American Philosophical Society in Philadelphia. Edward Everett, a professor of Greek, devoted his Phi Beta Kappa address at Harvard College in 1824 to a discussion of "The Circumstances Favorable to the Progress of Literature in America." In 1825 eighteen-year-old Henry Wadsworth Longfellow spoke of "Our Native Writers" in his commencement oration at Bowdoin College in Maine. In 1826 William Cullen Bryant delivered before the New York Athenaeum a series of four lectures on poetry that have been considered a milestone in the expression of American critical thought. William Ellery Channing's "The Importance and Means of a National Literature," published in the *Christian Examiner* of Boston in 1830, laid the groundwork for Ralph Waldo Emerson's ringing declaration of literary independence seven years later. In his address on "The American Scholar" delivered before the Phi Beta Kappa Society at Harvard on August 31, 1837, Emerson confidently asserted: "We will walk on our own feet; we will work with our own hands; we will speak our own minds."

Meanwhile, during this period apparently only one course dealing even in part with American literature was offered in an American college, and it, a series of "Lectures in American and English Literature" announced in 1827 at Amherst College, was dropped from the curriculum after two years of trial. In 1829 Samuel L. Knapp published *Lectures on American Literature; Some Remarks on Some Passages of American History*, the first attempt to put before the public a consecutive overview of native writings. Although excerpts from American authors had appeared since shortly after the Revolution in Noah Webster's popular "blue back" schoolbooks and American writers had been represented in several popular anthologies, the first school text to attempt a history of American literature was James R. Boyd's *Elements of Rhetoric and Literary Criticism . . . Including, also, A Succinct History of the English Language and of British and American Literature from the Earliest Times to the Present* in 1845. Three years later, Middlebury College offered two courses, one on "Critiques of British and American Classics (Poetry and Prose)," the other an "Analysis of American Orators." But elsewhere, interest in the subject developed slowly. In 1855 the two-volume *The Cyclopaedia of American Literature*, edited by Evert A. and George L. Duyckinck, was put together by nationalistic young men in New York. It was intended not as a college text, but as an exhibit to demonstrate that there was indeed a native tradition in letters. It is still a storehouse of early literary lore. In 1858, however, Heidelberg College in Ohio announced a course on "American Authors, Original Orators," and thereafter interest in native literature gradually grew. In the dozen years following the Civil War, American literature or some aspect of it was mentioned in the catalogues of twenty-six American colleges.

During the 1870s the subject began to flourish in small but important ways. In 1872 John Seely Hart of Princeton offered a course in American literature that was one of seven courses required of seniors for graduation. During the next year, Hart's *A Manual of American Literature*, the first book on the subject specifically designed as a college text, appeared. Two years later Moses Coit Tyler taught two courses in American literature at the University of Michigan, and in 1878 he published *A History of American Literature, 1607–1765*, the first scholarly study of American literary history and a work that, to this day, has not been superseded. In 1881 Tyler moved to Cornell University as a professor of American history and literature, where he continued to give courses, and in 1897 he produced *The Literary History of the American Revolution, 1763–1783*, another work that remains standard and authoritative.

The study of American literature now entered into a series of "firsts." The first inclusive survey of the subject was Charles E. Richardson's *American Literature, 1607–1885*, which appeared in two volumes in 1887 and 1888. The first course in American linguistics was offered at the University of Michigan in 1891. In 1894 the first doctoral dissertation in American literature was com pleted, a study of "Sources of Henry Wadsworth Longfellow's Poetry" by J. C. A. Schumacher at Yale University. In 1895, Lorenzo Sears of Brown University became the first professor of American literature; this was eight years before the first professorship in English literature was established in England at Oxford University and fifteen years before a professor of English literature was appointed at Cambridge.

During the early years of the twentieth century, a one-term course in American literature was offered, though irregularly, at Harvard University, but students of that period found greater attention given the subject at Yale and, especially, at Columbia University, which became an early center for American studies. The first course in the American short story was offered at the University of Oregon in 1911; the first course in American drama was announced at the University of Pennsylvania in 1917; in the same year, the first course on individual American writers—Poe, Emerson, and Whitman—was offered at the University of Oregon; and in 1920 the University of New Hampshire gave the first course in the American novel. A large step forward was taken in 1920 when the Modern Language Association of America authorized the formation of an American Literature Group among its members. In 1923 Middlebury College established the first separate and distinct department of American literature.

Meanwhile, both within and without the colleges and universities, interest in American writers and American literary history had been increasing. In 1900 Lewis E. Gates published mature critical estimates of familiar nineteenth-century writers, mostly from New England, in his *Studies and Appreciations;* Barrett Wendell from Harvard issued his somewhat pontifical and also New England-oriented *A Literary History of America;* and the popular poet and critic Edmund C. Stedman put together a large collection of native poetry in *An American Anthology, 1787–1900.* In 1901 James L. Onderdonk issued his still useful *History of American Verse, 1610–1897;* in 1902 Alonzo Sears's *American Literature in the Colonial and National Periods* appeared; and in 1903 were published William Peterfield Trent's intelligently critical *A History of American Literature, 1607–*

1865 and George E. Woodberry's somewhat more tendentious *America in Literature,* which gave slight attention either to Walt Whitman or to Mark Twain.

Something of a critical revolution was started by John Macy in 1908, when in his *The Spirit of American Literature* he urged that less attention be paid to the traditional poets of New England and more attention be shown to literary activities in regions other than New England and to distinctively indigenous writers such as Henry David Thoreau, Walt Whitman, and Mark Twain. William C. Brownell's *American Prose Masters* of 1909 is still read with appreciative respect, as is William B. Cairns' more pedestrian but inclusive *A History of American Literature,* which appeared in 1912. Interest in native literature was burgeoning, and American readers began to look with pride on native authors who filled the magazines and bookshops with writings that seemed as good and as polite as those produced anywhere. But in most colleges, American literature continued to be viewed as an adjunct to English literature, a poor relative posturing in borrowed transatlantic clothes.

After World War I, a smouldering fire of distrust among younger readers toward literature that was merely imitative and polite was fed by the new realism of such writers as Theodore Dreiser, Sherwood Anderson, and Eugene O'Neill. This fire was fanned to a bright blaze by the iconoclastic criticism of H. L. Mencken, first in *Smart Set,* then in the *American Mercury,* much of it collected in the six volumes of his *Prejudices* (1919–1927). Young men like Van Wyck Brooks, who in 1915 had looked with hardheaded hope toward *America's Coming of Age,* called for a reevaluation of American literature, and calls also went out for increased attention to it in the colleges and universities. In 1918 Benjamin Brawley broke new ground with *The Negro in Literature and Art in the United States.*

The publication from 1917 to 1921 of the four volumes of *The Cambridge History of American Literature,* edited by William Peterfield Trent, John Erskine, Stuart P. Sherman, and Carl Van Doren, has been called a landmark in the study and history of American letters, though the modern student may find many of its chapters more appropriate for the history they contain than for what they say about literature. A group of younger scholars who contributed to *The Reinterpretation of American Literature: Some*

*Contributions Toward the Understanding of Its Historical Develop-
ment* (1928) called for a new look at native letters, a more scholarly
literary approach, and a more realistic historical view.

But the watershed year in the development of American literary
studies was 1929, when, organized and managed by much this
same group of younger scholars, the first issue of *American Literature:
A Journal of Literary History, Criticism, and Bibliography*—a
quarterly that continues to be devoted exclusively to the study of
native letters—appeared from Duke University. Jay B. Hubbell, its
founding editor and until 1954 the chairman of its editorial board,
tells in his delightfully reminiscent *South and Southwest* (Durham,
N.C.: Duke Univ. Press, 1965) [PS121/H83] of the struggles
during the early 1920s as this group of young academicians battled
to achieve recognition for the study of American literature. He tells
of smoke-filled meetings, long as only deeply concerned professors
can lengthen them, in which strategies were worked out, plans
formulated, and, finally, results achieved.

Those who joined Hubbell in this enterprise were truly dedicated
and heroic people, whose names should not be forgotten: William
B. Cairns of the University of Wisconsin; Killis Campbell of the
University of Texas; Norman Foerster of the University of North
Carolina; Kenneth B. Murdock of Harvard University; Louise
Pound of the University of Nebraska; Arthur Hobson Quinn of the
University of Pennsylvania; Ralph Leslie Rusk of Columbia Uni-
versity; and Stanley T. Williams of Yale University. They were
encouraged by such older scholars as William Peterfield Trent, re-
cently of Columbia University, Fred Lewis Pattee, retired from
Pennsylvania State College, and Henry Seidel Canby, who had left
teaching at Yale University to edit the *Saturday Review of Literature;*
and they were spurred on by the youngest of them all, Robert E.
Spiller, then of Swarthmore College. Together with John Seely
Hart and Moses Coit Tyler, these men are among the scholar-
teachers who have been responsible for the recognition in the
academic community of American literature as a subject worthy of
study as a reputable part of the college curriculum.

During the last fifty years, the study and teaching of American
literature have greatly increased; the subject is now recognized as
legitimate, and important, in virtually every college and university
in the United States—and in foreign universities on each of the five

continents. After World War II, largely through the active advocacy of Robert E. Spiller, then at the University of Pennsylvania, the study of American literature was often joined with the study of other expressions of the American spirit—its art, architecture, music, and politics—into a newer discipline, especially popular abroad, called American Studies. Most modern students of our literature, however, while they have learned to view it in relation to other aspects of native and foreign culture, prefer to approach it as an important thing in itself.

Since 1929 students of American literature have been engaged in a kind of literary housekeeping, putting their residence more neatly in order, attempting to make it more attractive to those who would stop to visit. Literary history has been rewritten several times, sometimes from an intellectual or regional bias, and sometimes through collaborative enterprises that have assumed that several minds were better to be trusted than one. Bibliographies, indexes, and finding-lists have been devised. Writers seldom mentioned before, like Edward Taylor and Kate Chopin, have been elevated to prominence. Characters who an earlier generation had not always considered worthy of literary recognition, like Huckleberry Finn and Sut Lovingood, have been admitted to serious discussion. Biographers have been especially busy, sometimes writing at such length and in such detail that they have been accused of telling a reader more than he really wants to know about a writer—or telling a critic more than he finds intellectually or aesthetically useful. Private presses and quality publishers have produced beautifully designed limited editions of favorite volumes by American writers. Complete editions of the writings of important American authors have been projected, each to be prepared under rigorous supervision according to precise textual principles set up by the Center for Editions of American Authors, which is sponsored by the Modern Language Association of America and funded by the National Endowment for the Humanities. These editions are intended to allow the reader to discover exactly what the author had planned to say before carelessness or censorship corrupted it.

Meanwhile, literary criticism has burgeoned in many guises. Excitement has been generated as critics (sometimes facetiously called "crickits") of one persuasion have battled critics of other orientations. Fresh insights and new and stimulating interpretations have been revealed. On the whole, literature has increasingly been examined as literature, not as tract, sermon, or merely historical artifact. And now the care and nurture of American literature first evidenced more than two hundred years ago by undergraduates in American colleges becomes the custodial inheritance of modern American students.

CHAPTER TWO
Literary Histories

GENERAL SURVEYS

Histories of American literature that appeared during the 1930s were likely to describe their subject matter as interesting for reasons other than the fact that it was literature. Once valued as a stimulating interpretation because of its author's conviction that social and economic forces determine directions that literature inevitably follows, Vernon Louis Parrington's *Main Currents in American Thought: An Interpretation of American Literature from the Beginnings to 1920,** 3 vols. (New York: Harcourt, Brace, 1927–

* An asterisk indicates that the title is available in a paperback edition.

1930) [PS88/P3] is less highly thought of now because of alleged failures in moral and aesthetic judgments. V. F. Calverton's *The Liberation of American Literature* (New York: Scribner's, 1932) [PS88/C26] presents an interesting Marxist interpretation but must not be depended on for factual information. A more reliable expression of a Marxist view is Granville Hicks, *The Great Tradition: An Interpretation of American Literature Since the Civil War*, rev. ed. (New York: Macmillan, 1933) [PS214/H5/1935]; see also his *Proletarian Literature in the United States: An Anthology* (New York: International Publishers, 1935) [PS509/P7P7]. A Freudian view is set forth in Ludwig Lewisohn, *Expressionism in America* (1932), a revised edition of which appeared as *The Story of American Literature* (New York: Harper, 1937) [PS88/L45/1937].

More deliberative studies that appeared in the 1930s are Henry Seidel Canby, *Classic Americans: A Study of Eminent American Writers from Irving to Whitman, with an Introductory Survey of the Colonial Background of Our National Literature* (New York: Harcourt, Brace, 1931) [PS88/C35], and Walter F. Taylor, *A History of American Letters* (1936), expanded to *The Story of American Letters* (Chicago: Regnery, 1956) [PS88/T3/1956]. Russell Blankenship, *American Literature As an Expression of the National Mind*, rev. ed. (New York: Holt, Rinehart & Winston, 1958) [PS88/B58/1958], though deriving from Parrington, contains balanced independent and sound literary judgments. Fred Lewis Pattee, *The First Century of American Literature, 1770–1870* (New York and London: Appleton-Century, 1935) [PS88/P35] completed a three-volume survey that included *A History of American Literature Since 1870* (New York: Century, 1915) [PS214/P3] and *The New American Literature, 1890–1930* (New York and London: Century, 1930) [PS221/P3].

A longer and less formal survey, impressionistic, sometimes derivative, but always readable, is Van Wyck Brooks, *Makers and Finders: A History of the Writer in America, 1800–1915* (New York: Dutton, 1936–1952], which appeared in five volumes; in order of the periods covered, they are: *The World of Washington Irving* (1944) [PS208/B7]; *The Flowering of New England, 1815–1965* (1936), with a new and revised edition appearing a year later [PS243/B7/1937]; *The Times of Melville and Whitman* (1947)

[PS201/B7]; *New England: Indian Summer, 1865–1915* (1940) [PS243/B72/1940]; and *The Confident Years, 1885–1915* (1952) [PS214/B7].

In 1948 the collaborative *Literary History of the United States*, edited by Robert E. Spiller, Willard Thorp, Thomas H. Johnson, and Henry Seidel Canby, assisted in later editions by Richard M. Ludwig and William M. Gibson, first appeared; the 4th edition, revised, of this work is the best for student use (New York: Macmillan; London: Collier-Macmillan, 1974) [PS88/L522/1974]. Usually referred to as the *LHUS*, the first volume contains chapters on literary history contributed by sixty scholars, transitions between chapters being supplied by paragraphs prepared by the editors. Individual chapters vary in usefulness, but the work as a whole is a useful and extensive interpretation well worth consulting. The second volume contains bibliographies and has been separately issued (see "Bibliographical Guides," p. 64 below).

Also uneven is *The Literature of the American People: An Historical and Critical Survey*, edited by Arthur Hobson Quinn (New York: Appleton-Century-Crofts, 1951) [PS88/Q5], which contains extensive essays by five distinguished American scholars. Kenneth B. Murdock of Harvard is somewhat old-fashioned in his treatment of "The Colonial and Revolutionary Period," failing to take into consideration some of the then more recent scholarship in that area. Arthur Hobson Quinn of the University of Pennsylvania, in writing of "The Establishment of National Literature," does not adequately evaluate the important achievements of Walt Whitman and Herman Melville. By far the most original and informative section is the one by Clarence Gohdes of Duke University; what he has to say about "The Later Nineteenth Century" is controlled by a firm, well-informed grasp of literary history, particularly in his introductory chapter on "The Age of the Monthly Magazine." What George F. Whicher of Amherst College has to say on "The Twentieth Century" has been largely superseded by later authorities.

Howard Mumford Jones, *O Strange New World: American Culture, The Formative Years* (New York: Viking, 1964) [E169/ 1/E162] and its sequels, *Revolution and Romanticism* (Cambridge: Belknap Press of Harvard Univ. Press, 1974) [CB411/J66] and *The Age of Energy: Varieties of American Experience, 1865–1915*

(New York: Viking, 1971) [E169/1/J6435], present the most informed overview of American culture put together by a single author, especially concerning the relationships of that culture to native and transatlantic intellectual trends. Jones is among the foremost living American scholars. What he says is said with authority. People who have attempted to contradict him have almost always come to grief, for he is almost always right. His *The Theory of American Literature,* reissued with a new concluding chapter (Ithaca, N.Y.: Cornell Univ. Press, 1965) [PA31/J6/1965] is a classic brief study of the ideas that lie behind much of the best American writing from colonial times to the present.

Transitions in American Literary History, edited by Harry Hayden Clark for the American Literature Group of the Modern Language Association of America (Durham, N.C.: Duke Univ. Press, 1953) [PS88/C6], contains essays by seven prominent scholars on periods in the history of American literature, with special emphasis on changes in intellectual and aesthetic attitudes; of special and almost unique value is the essay by Leon Howard on "The Late Eighteenth Century: An Age of Contradiction." Edmund Wilson, *The Shock of Recognition: The Development of Literature in the United States Recorded by the Men Who Made It,* 2 vols., rev. ed. (New York: Farrar, Straus and Cudahy, 1955) [PS55/W5/1955] presents a provocative collection of statements about American writers made by other distinguished American writers, including Wilson himself.

Though not a comprehensive literary history, Tony Tanner, *The Reign of Wonder: Naivety and Reality in American Literature* (Cambridge: Cambridge Univ. Press, 1965) [PS88/T25] points to attitudes of wonder and deliberate naivety among the early nineteenth-century transcendentalists, attitudes that developed through the writings of Mark Twain to those of Gertrude Stein, Sherwood Anderson, and Ernest Hemingway in the creation of a distinctively American style. But Robert E. Spiller, *The Cycle of American Literature** (New York: Macmillan, 1955) [PS88/S6] derived from the *LHUS,* though partially marred by a problematical theory of cyclical development, remains perhaps the most useful overall survey contained in a single volume. Its facts are correct, but the application of them to Spiller's cyclical theory is thought by some critics to be faulty; others, however, agree with him almost completely: that, it can be said, is what makes horse racing, and scholarship also, often exciting.

PERIOD STUDIES

The standard history of colonial American literature remains Moses Coit Tyler, *A History of American Literature during the Colonial Period*, 2 vols., rev. ed. (New York: G. P. Putnam's Sons, 1897) [PS185/T8/1897]. It can be supplemented by Thomas G. Wright, *Literary Culture in Early New England, 1620–1730* (New Haven: Yale Univ. Press, 1920) [F7/W95]; Kenneth B. Murdock, *Literature and Theology in Colonial New England* (Cambridge: Harvard Univ. Press, 1949) [PS195/R4M8]; Samuel Eliot Morison, *The Intellectual Life of Colonial New England** (Cambridge: Harvard Univ. Press, 1956) [F7/M82/1956], first published in 1939 as *The Puritan Pronaos*; but especially by Perry Miller, *The New England Mind: The Seventeenth Century** (Cambridge: Harvard Univ. Press, 1939) [F7/M56] and *The New England Mind: From Colony to Province** (Cambridge: Harvard Univ. Press, 1953) [F7/M54], both of which are important milestones in intellectual history. Russel Nye, *American Literary History, 1607–1830** (New York: Knopf, 1970) [PS88/N9] is a brief and, in most instances, reliable survey.

A generous anthology of colonial New England writing, with excellent introductions and helpful bibliographies, is Perry Miller and Thomas H. Johnson, eds., *The Puritans*, rev. ed. (New York: Harper & Row, 1963) [PS531/M5/1963]. Two useful anthologies of early verse are Kenneth Silverman, ed., *Colonial American Poetry* (New York: Hafner, 1968) [PS601/S5], which is discriminatingly selective and contains excellent critical commentary, and Harrison T. Meserole, ed., *Seventeenth-Century American Poetry* (New York: New York Univ. Press, 1968) [PS601/M4/1968a], which is more traditional and less selective.

The beginnings of a national literature are so well detailed in Moses Coit Tyler, *The Literary History of the American Revolution, 1763–1783* (New York: G. P. Putnam's Sons, 1897) [PS185/T82] that few have ventured to improve on it.

Excellent studies of literary activities in specific places and regions are Carl and Jessica Bridenbaugh, *Rebels and Gentlemen: Phila-delphia in the Age of Franklin** (New York: Reynal & Hitchcock, 1942) [F158/4/B6], and Richard Beale Davis, *Intellectual Life in Jefferson's Virginia, 1790–1830* (Chapel Hill: Univ. of North Carolina Press, 1964) [F230/D3]. Lewis Leary, *Soundings: Some Early American Writers* (Athens: Univ. of Georgia Press, 1975) [PS193/L4] is a collection of fourteen essays on writers from Benjamin Franklin to James Fenimore Cooper and Washington Irving. Covering both the colonial and the early national periods, Everett Emerson, ed., *Major Writers of Early American Literature* (Madison: Univ. of Wisconsin Press, 1972) [PS185/E24] contains eight essays on literary pioneers from William Bradford to Charles Brockden Brown.

There is no completely satisfactory survey of literature of the early national period, from the end of the American Revolution to the appearance of Edgar Allan Poe and Ralph Waldo Emerson in the second and third decades of the nineteenth century, though at least three are currently in progress; see, however, Russel B. Nye, *The Cultural Life of the New Nation, 1776–1830** (New York: Harper, 1960) [E169/1/N9], Van Wyck Brooks, *The World of Washington Irving* and Howard Mumford Jones, *Revolution and Romanticism* (see pp. 12–13 and 13–14, above).

The period of the emergence of what was to become a truly national literature is surveyed in Van Wyck Brooks, *The Times of Melville and Whitman* (see pp. 12–13, above). Perry Miller, *The Raven and the Whale: The War of Words and Wits in the Era of Poe and Melville* (New York: Harcourt, Brace, 1956) [PS74/M5] examines the activities of young men, principally in New York, who battled among themselves in an attempt to determine what a genuinely national native literature should be. Chief among the values of this book is its examination of writers, prominent in their time but now almost forgotten, who nonetheless created a literary atmosphere that encouraged the talents of writers like Edgar Allan Poe, Nathaniel Hawthorne, and Herman Melville. Miller provides a judicious overview of literary activity during the formative years of our literature, but his book must be checked for accuracy of detail against John Stafford, *The Literary Criticism of "Young America": A Study of the Relationship of Politics and Literature,*

1837–1850 (Berkeley: Univ. of California Press, 1952) [PN99/U5S7].

A major work in literary scholarship, and perhaps the single most influential study of literature in America at the middle of the nineteenth century, is F. O. Matthiessen, *American Renaissance: Art and Expression in the Age of Emerson and Whitman* (New York: Oxford Univ. Press, 1941) [PS261/M3]. Matthiessen discovers a fusion of form and content in such important books of the 1850s as Ralph Waldo Emerson's *Representative Men* (1850), Nathaniel Hawthorne's *The Scarlet Letter* (1850) and *The House of the Seven Gables* (1851), Herman Melville's *Moby-Dick* (1851) and *Pierre* (1852), Henry David Thoreau's *Walden* (1854), and Walt Whitman's *Leaves of Grass* (1855). He explains what there was in the cultural situation of the United States that made these books possible during that six-year period.

Matthiessen examines these books and writers in the context of their time, in their relationships to other arts in America, in their importance as writers and works that established patterns and attitudes which would influence later writing, and, most important, in defining the attitudes held "by these four of our major writers concerning the function and nature of literature, and the degree to which their practice bore out their theories." *American Renaissance* is a seminal book that has radically influenced the direction of American literary studies: it is criticism at its alert and far-reaching best, held carefully within the requirements of literary history; it is literary history comprehensively conceived as an instrument for effective literary criticism. Speaking as it does of the first great surge toward the creation of a national literature, it has become a book that every student of that literature keeps by his side, for rereading and for reference.

Deriving in part from the influence of Matthiessen is R. W. B. Lewis, *The American Adam: Innocence, Tradition and Tragedy in the Nineteenth Century* (Chicago: Univ. of Chicago Press, 1955) [PS201/L4], a study of the history of ideas and especially of the clusters of ideas discovered among the kinds of images and narratives prevalent during the middle of the nineteenth century. Though principally concerned with defining the Adamic quest—the attempt by American writers to view the world as if for the first time, without dependence on tradition—Lewis's book is often best remembered for its perhaps too facile division of writers of that period into three "parties," (1) the party of memory or of history that is represented by such writers as John Greenleaf Whittier and Henry Wadsworth Longfellow, (2) the party of hope led by Ralph Waldo Emerson and Walt Whitman, and (3) the party of doubt dominated by Nathaniel Hawthorne and Herman Melville. It is, however, a thoughtful, provocative book that explores many of the intellectual crosscurrents which livened an important period in the development of literature in America.

Principal among those currents was transcendentalism, which flowed from New England throughout much of the United States, attracting ardent advocates and equally ardent, sometimes mocking, opponents. The difficult problem of determining just what transcendentalism was can be partially solved by consulting such standard works as Octavius B. Frothingham, *Transcendentalism in New England: A History* (New York: G. P. Putnam, 1870; rpt., New York: Harper, 1959) [B905/F7/1959] and Harold Clark Goddard, *Studies in New England Transcendentalism* (New York: Columbia Univ. Press, 1908) [B905/G6]. But the idea is perhaps best clarified in Perry Miller, ed., *The Transcendentalists: An Anthology** (Cambridge: Harvard Univ. Press, 1950) [B905/M5], which reprints definitions, defenses, and apologies made by advocates of that philosophy. Paul F. Boller, Jr., *American Transcendentalism, 1830–1860: An Intellectual Inquiry* (New York: Putnam, 1974) [B994/N8/B6] is a readable short survey of the main themes of the movement, viewing it as both religious and philosophical and as a spur to cosmic optimism.

Edmund Wilson, *Patriotic Gore: Studies in the Literature of the American Civil War* (New York: Oxford Univ. Press, 1962) [PS211/W5] is an uneven but seminal study of writers who were popular and influential in their own time but who have been overlooked by many modern critics. Grant C. Knight, *The Critical Period in American Literature* (Chapel Hill: Univ. of North Carolina Press, 1951) [PS214/K6] examines the movement toward a realistic literature that began to gain momentum at the close of the Civil War. Much the same period is covered in greater detail in Jay Martin, *Harvests of Change: American Literature, 1865–1914* (Englewood Cliffs, N.J.: Prentice-Hall, 1967) [PS214/M35], which explains how literature reflected the transformations that took place as America expanded in technology, wealth, and territory in the period between the Civil War and World War I. See also Fred Lewis Pattee, *A History of American Literature Since 1870;* Van Wyck Brooks, *New England Summer, 1865–1915* and *The Confident Years, 1885–1915;* Clarence Gohdes, "The Later Nineteenth Century," in *The Literature of the American People,* ed. Arthur Hobson Quinn; and Howard Mumford Jones, *The Age of Energy: Varieties of American Experience, 1865–1915* (see p. 12, pp. 13–14, above). Larzer Ziff, *The American 1890's: Life and Times of a Lost Generation* (New York: Viking, 1966) [PS214/Z5] tells of writers who helped set the stage for developments in literature in the twentieth century.

There is no adequate complete survey of twentieth-century American literature, though there are several excellent studies of fiction, poetry, and drama (see "Studies in Genre," below). Anyone who will search through the forest of writing on the literature of this century will discover pathways made clear in Howard Mumford Jones and Richard M. Ludwig, eds., *Guide to American Literature and Its Backgrounds Since 1890,* 4th ed. (Cambridge: Harvard Univ. Press, 1972) [Z1225/J65/1972].

REGIONAL SURVEYS

After the Civil War, as America expanded westward and attempted to mend the wounds suffered by the South, new centers of literature developed in the West, the Midwest, and the revived South. Each has attracted historians, who have often devotedly and at length explained why the region of which they write has been or still is important in the creation of a literature of which all Americans may be proud.

Writing in New England and the Middle Atlantic states, where literature during much of the nineteenth century flourished most consistently, is reviewed in almost all the general surveys and period studies mentioned above. Perry D. Westbrook, *Acres of Flint: Writers of Rural New England, 1870–1900* (Washington, D.C.: Scarecrow, 1951) [PS243/W4] speaks interestingly of several local-color writers who are not often noticed at length in standard literary histories.

Histories of literary activities in the western United States include Franklin Walker, *San Francisco's Literary Frontier** (New York: Knopf, 1939) [PS285/S3W3] and his *A Literary History of Southern California* (Berkeley: Univ. of California Press, 1939) [PS383/C2W3]; and Kevin Starr, *Americans and the California Dream 1850–1915* (New York: Oxford Univ. Press, 1973) [F861/582]. These, however, should be supplemented by the broader studies of Lucy Hazard, *The Frontier in American Literature* (New York: Crowell, 1927) [PS169/F7H3]; Edwin Fussell, *Frontier: American Literature and the American West* (Princeton: Princeton Univ. Press, 1965) [PS169/W4F8]; and Robert Edson Lee, *From East to West: Studies in the Literature of the American West* (Urbana: Univ. of Illinois Press, 1966) [PS374/W4L4]. Henry Nash Smith, *Virgin Land: The American West as Symbol and Myth* (Cambridge: Harvard Univ. Press, 1950) [F591/S65] is a standard and trailblazing explanation of how various conceptions of the West have influenced American literature in fact and symbol.

On the Midwest, Ralph Leslie Rusk, *The Literature of the Middle Western Frontier,* 2 vols. (New York: Columbia Univ. Press, 1925) [PS273/R8] is an important thorough survey, though more useful for its bibliographical references than for its sometimes laboriously detailed text. More readable but less complete is Dorothy Dondore, *The Prairie and the Making of Middle America* (Cedar Rapids, Iowa: Torch, 1926) [F351/D67]. Literature of the American Southwest is surveyed in Mabel Major and others, *Southwest Heritage: A Literary History with Bibliography,* 3rd ed. (Albuquerque: Univ. of New Mexico Press, 1972) [PS277/M3/1972]; see also J. Frank Dobie, *Guide to the Life and Literature of the Southwest,* rev. ed. (Dallas: Southern Methodist Univ. Press, 1952) [Z1251/S8D6].

Southern literature has been surveyed in great detail, especially recently; see Louis D. Rubin, Jr., ed., *A Bibliographical Guide to the Study of Southern Literature* (Baton Rouge: Louisiana State Univ. Press, 1969) [Z1225/S6R8], supplemented since 1969 by annual checklists published in spring issues of the *Mississippi Quarterly.* The standard work is Jay B. Hubbell, *The South in American Literature, 1607–1900* (Durham, N.C.: Duke Univ. Press, 1954) [PS261/H78], which is a detailed, authoritative, historical and biographical account. An indispensable compendium of facts, the book represents a lifetime of scholarly inquiry and is especially detailed in explaining antebellum trends and writers.

Early literature of the South is described in Howard Mumford Jones, *The Literature of Virginia in the Seventeenth Century*, 2d ed. (Charlottesville: Univ. Press of Virginia, 1968) [PS266/V5J6]; Richard Beale Davis, *Intellectual Life in Jefferson's Virginia, 1790–1830* (Chapel Hill: Univ. of North Carolina Press, 1964) [F230/D3]; and J. A. Leo Lemay, *Men of Letters in Colonial Maryland* (Knoxville: Univ. of Tennessee Press, 1972) [PS266/M3L4]. For later writers, see Louis D. Rubin, Jr., and Robert D. Jacobs, *Southern Renascence: The Literature of the Modern South* (Baltimore: Johns Hopkins Press, 1953) [PS261/R67]; their *South: Modern Southern Literature in Its Cultural Setting* (Garden City: Doubleday, 1951) [PS261/R65]; and Rubin, *The Faraway Country: Writers of the Modern South* (Seattle: Univ. of Washington Press, 1963) [PS261/R63]. C. Hugh Holman has examined the nature of southern writing, past and present, in "The Southerner As American Writer," in *The Southerner as American*, ed. Charles Grier Sellers (Chapel Hill: Univ. of North Carolina Press, 1960) [F209/S44]; also in "A Cycle of Change in Southern Literature," in *The South in Continuity and Change*, ed. John C. McKinney and Edgar T. Thompson (Durham, N.C.: Duke Univ. Press, 1965) [HN79/A13M214]; and with special acuity in his *Three Modes of Southern Fiction* (Athens: Univ. of Georgia Press, 1968) [PS379/H64].

Allen Tate's *Collected Essays* (Denver: Swallow, 1959) [PN37/T27] has been described as a work that everyone seriously concerned with southern literature should examine, because it contains in germ or detail every idea that modern commentators have found fruitful. Also informative are Frederick J. Hoffman, *The Art of Southern Fiction* (Carbondale: Southern Illinois Univ. Press, 1967) [PS261/H48]; Edd Winfield Parks, *Ante-Bellum Southern Literary Critics* (Athens: Univ. of Georgia Press, 1962) [PN99/U52P3], and his *Southern Poets: Representative Selections* (New York: American Book Company, 1936) [PS551/P27], which contains an excellent bibliography; Arthur Palmer Hudson, *Humor of the Old Deep South* (New York: Macmillan, 1936) [PN6158/H75]; M. Thomas Inge, *The Frontier Humorists: Critical Views* (Hamden, Conn.: Archon, 1975) [PS430/I5]; and James H. Dormon, Jr., *Theater in the Ante-Bellum South, 1815–1861* (Chapel Hill: Univ. of North Carolina Press, 1967) [PN2248/D6].

ETHNIC LITERATURE

Serious historic and evaluative criticism of American writing from the point of view of the ethnic experience is a very recent development in scholarship, even though some of the groundwork was laid in two 1948 essays contributed to the *Literary History of the United States*: "The Mingling of Tongues" by Henry A. Pochmann and "The Indian Heritage" by Stith Thompson, both reprinted in the 4th ed., rev. (New York: Macmillan, 1974) [PS88/L522/1974]. Most of the writing has been focused on the contributions of black Americans, although other ethnic groups are now being studied as well. The most complete survey of fiction written by blacks is Robert A. Bone, *The Negro Novel in America*, rev. ed. (New Haven: Yale Univ. Press, 1965) [PS153/N5B5], which has been extended and supplemented by further studies such as those by Edward Margolies, *Native Sons: A Critical Study of Twentieth-Century Negro American Authors* (Philadelphia: Lippincott, 1968) [PS508/N3M3]; Nathan Irvin Huggins, *Harlem Renaissance* (New York: Oxford Univ. Press, 1971) [NX512.3/N5H5]; and Roger Rosenblatt, *Black Fiction* (Cambridge: Harvard Univ. Press, 1974) [PS374/N4R6]. A radical call for a more racially oriented criticism of black literature can be found in the essays collected by Addison Gayle in *The Black Aesthetic* (Garden City: Doubleday, 1971) [NX512.3/N5G38]. See also Edith J. R. Isaacs, *The Negro in the American Theatre* (New York: Theatre Arts Books, 1947) [PN2286/I8]; Benjamin Griffith Brawley, *The Negro in Literature and Art in the United States*, rpt. (St. Claire Shores, Mich.: Scholarly, 1972) [PS153/N5/B65]; and Blyden Jackson and Louis D. Rubin, Jr., *Black Poetry in America: Two Essays in Interpretation* (Baton Rouge: Louisiana State Univ. Press, 1974) [PS153/N5/J3].

Full-length studies of Jewish-American writing include Solomon Liptzin, *The Jew in American Literature* (New York: Bloch, 1966) [PS173/J4L5]; Robert Alter, *After the Tradition: Essays on Modern Jewish Writing* (New York: Dutton, 1969) [PJ5017/A4]; Max F.

Schulz, *Radical Sophistication: Studies in Contemporary Jewish-American Novelists* (Athens: Ohio Univ. Press, 1969) [PS379/ S394]; and Allen Guttmann, *The Jewish Writer in America—Assimilation and the Crisis of Identity* (New York: Oxford Univ. Press, 1971) [PS153/J4G8]. While comprehensive critical studies of the writings of other ethnic groups have not yet appeared, the introductions, bibliographies, and critical notes in the following anthologies will prove of great help to the researcher: Lillian Faderman and Barbara Bradshaw, eds., *Speaking for Ourselves* (Glenview, Ill.: Scott, Foresman, 1969) [PE1122/F3]; Luis Valdez and Stan Steiner, eds., *Aztlan: An Anthology of Mexican-American Literature* (New York: Knopf, 1972) [E184/M5V3]; Frank Chin and others, eds., *Aiiieeeee! An Anthology of Asian-American Writers* (Washington, D.C.: Howard Univ. Press, 1974) [PS508/A8A4]; Shirley Hill Witt and Stan Steiner, eds., *The Way: An Anthology of American Indian Literature* (New York: Knopf, 1972) [PM197/E1W5]; Jerome Rothenberg, ed., *Shaking the Pumpkin: Traditional Poetry of the Indian North Americas* (Garden City: Doubleday, 1972) [PM197/ E3R6]; Thomas E. Sanders and Walter W. Peek, eds., *Literature of the North American Indian* (Beverly Hills, Ca.: Glencoe, 1973) [PM197/E1S2]; Gloria Levitas and others, eds., *American Indian Prose and Poetry* (New York: G. P. Putnam's Sons, 1974) [PM197/ E1L4]; and Frederick W. Turner, III, ed., *The Portable North American Indian Reader* (New York: Viking, 1974) [E77/T937/ 1974]. In 1974 the Society for the Study of the Multi-Ethnic Literature of the United States was formed to encourage and support further examination of America's literary and cultural ethnic diversity.

INTELLECTUAL TRENDS

Students who are interested in intellectual trends and movements will want to supplement Parrington with such books as Merle Curti, *The Growth of American Thought*, 3rd ed. (New York: Harper & Row, 1964) [E169/1/C87/1964] or Woodbridge Riley, *American Thought from Puritanism to Pragmatism*, 2d ed. (New York: Holt, 1923) [B851/R5/1923]. Clifton E. Olmstead, *History of Religion*

In America (Englewood Cliffs, N.J.: Prentice-Hall, 1960) [BR515/ 04] is an invaluable, well-informed guide that contains useful bibliographical references. Popular attitudes viewed historically and discussed in terms helpful to the student of literature will be found in Richard Hofstadter, *Social Darwinism in American Thought*, rev. ed. (Boston: Beacon, 1955) [HM22/U5H6/1955]; Louis Hartz, *The Liberal Tradition in America: An Interpretation of American Political Thought Since the Revolution* (New York: Harcourt, Brace, 1955) [E175/H37]; Clinton L. Rossiter, *Conservatism in America: The Thankless Persuasion*, 2d ed. (New York: Knopf, 1962) [JK31/R58/1962]; Donald Drew Egbert and Stow Persons, eds., *Socialism and American Life*, 2 vols. (Princeton: Princeton Univ. Press, 1952) [HX83/E45]; and Stow Persons, ed., *Evolutionary Thought in America* (New Haven: Yale Univ. Press, 1950; New York: Braziller, 1956) [B818/P4], the last two of which are symposiums and also supply useful bibliographies. Eleanor Flexner, *Century of Struggle: The Woman's Rights Movement in the United States** (Cambridge: Belknap Press of Harvard Univ. Press, 1959) [HQ1410/F6] will inevitably be supplemented, but not replaced, by further studies now in preparation. Albert Parry, *Garrets and Pretenders: A History of Bohemianism in America,** rev. ed. (New York: Dover, 1960) [PS138/P3/1960] contains as its final chapter a history of the beatniks by Harry T. Moore. Daniel Aaron, *Writers on the Left: Episodes in American Literary Communism* (New York: Harcourt, Brace & World, 1961) [PS228/C6A2] reveals the response of many American writers from 1912 to 1940 to the blandishments of Communist theory.

For material on transcendentalism, see "Period Studies," p. 18 above.

LITERARY TRENDS AND DEVICES

Literary scholars who have surveyed the development of American literature by tracing a theme, an idea, or a trend have included Ima Honaker Herron, *The Small Town in American Literature* (Durham, N.C.: Duke Univ. Press, 1939; rpt., New York: Pageant, 1959) [PS169/S5H4]; Howard W. Hintz, *The Quaker Influence on American Literature* (New York: Fleming H. Revell, 1940) [PS166/

H5]; and Floyd Stovall, *American Idealism* (Norman: Univ. of Oklahoma Press, 1943; rpt., Port Washington, N.Y.: Kennikat, 1965) [PS169/I3S3]. Edwin H. Cady, *The Gentleman in America: A Literary Study in American Culture* (Syracuse: Syracuse Univ. Press, 1949) [BJ1601/C2] can be read in conjunction with either William Wasserstrom, *Heiress of All the Ages: Sex and Sentiment in the Genteel Tradition* (Minneapolis: Univ. of Minnesota Press, 1959) [PS374/W6W3/1959] or the earlier Dixon Wecter, *The Hero in America: A Chronicle of Hero-Worship* (New York: Scribner's, 1941) [E176/W4]. Frederick W. Conner, *Cosmic Optimism: A Study of the Interpretation of Evolution by American Poets from Emerson to Robinson* (Gainesville: Univ. of Florida Press, 1949) [PS310/E8C6] and Benjamin T. Spenser, *The Quest for Nationality* (Syracuse: Syracuse Univ. Press, 1957) [PS88/558] are workmanlike studies that contain valuable information. Randall Stewart, *American Literature & Christian Doctrine* (Baton Rouge: Louisiana State Univ. Press, 1958) [PS166/S8] is worth looking at, if only to see how debatable criticism can sometimes be.

Charles Feidelson, *Symbolism and American Literature* (Chicago: Univ. of Chicago Press, 1953) [PS201/F4] calls attention to the prevalence and importance of symbolic representation in almost all American literature; see also William York Tindall, *The Literary Symbol* (New York: Columbia Univ. Press, 1955) [PS56/S9T5], which extends the consideration of symbolic devices to literatures other than American. R. W. B. Lewis, *The American Adam: Innocence, Tragedy, and Tradition in the Nineteenth Century* (see p. 18 above) [PS201/L4] explains the attempt by classic American writers to see the world as if, like Adam, they were seeing it for the first time. Leo Marx, *The Machine and the Garden: Technology and the Pastoral in America** (New York: Oxford Univ. Press, 1964) [E169/1/M35] finds that much of what has been most representative in American literature has resulted from attempts to resolve the tensions caused by opposing ideals. Quentin Anderson, *The Imperial Self: An Essay in American Literary and Cultural History* (New York: Knopf, 1971) [PS201/A5] finds that much failure in American writing has been the result of an author's paying more attention to his or her undirected self than in recognizing and building upon received literary traditions.

LITERATURE AND THE ARTS

Arts other than literature that have had an effect on literature can be conveniently surveyed in Oliver W. Larkin, *Art in America,* rev. ed. (New York: Holt, Rinehart & Winston, 1960) [N6505/L37/ 1960], which surveys the history of architecture, sculpture, painting, and other arts and offers a useful, detailed bibliography of other sources; and John T. Howard, *Our American Music: A Comprehensive History from 1620 to the Present,* 2d ed. (New York: McGraw-Hill, 1966) [ML200/C5]; see also John H. Mueller, *The American Symphony Orchestra: A Social History of Musical Taste* (Bloomington: Indiana Univ. Press, 1951) [ML200/M8]. Lewis Mumford, *The Brown Decades: A Study of the Arts in America, 1865–1895,* rev. ed. (New York: Dover, 1966) [N6510/M8/1955] is an informed and pleasantly written survey of the arts in various forms in the nineteenth century; Russell Lynes, *The Art-Makers of the Nineteenth Century* (New York: Atheneum, 1970) [N6505/L95] surveys both the fine and the practical arts.

John A. Kouwenhoven, *Made in America: the Arts in Modern Civilization* (Garden City: Doubleday, 1948) [N6505/K6] is an able literary scholar's explanation of how the arts, even popular arts and inventions, have influenced literary expression. His *The Beer Can by the Roadway: Essays on What Is American about America* (Garden City: Doubleday, 1961) [N6506/K8] sets forth a provocative theory, artfully expressed, that boldly classifies such American achievements as the skyscraper, chewing gum, the soap opera, progressive jazz, *Moby-Dick, Leaves of Grass,* and *Adventures of Huckleberry Finn* as manifestations of an American interest in "becoming" rather than "being," of endless movement, of going places, rather than of standing still.

POPULAR TASTE

Frank Luther Mott, *Golden Multitudes: The Story of Best Sellers in the United States* (New York: Macmillan, 1947) [Z1033/B3M6] reviews the vagaries of American taste from colonial times to the twentieth century. It may be supplemented by James D. Hart, *The*

Popular Book: A History of America's Literary Taste (New York: Oxford Univ. Press, 1950) [Z1003/H328] and by Jay B. Hubbell, *Who Are the Major American Writers? A Study of the Changing Literary Canon* (Durham, N.C.: Duke Univ. Press, 1972) [PS62/ H8]. Carl Bode, *The Anatomy of American Popular Culture, 1840– 1861* (Berkeley: Univ. of California Press, 1959) [E169/1/B657] reviews the popular fine arts and popular preferences in the years preceding the Civil War. William Charvat, *Literary Publishing in America, 1790–1850* (Philadelphia: Univ. of Pennsylvania Press, 1959) [PN155/C5] demonstrates how an entanglement of many discouraging hardships—such as lack of adequate copyright, difficulties in distribution, and inadequacies in public taste—made the making and selling of books often a risky occupation in early nineteenth-century America. Henry Nash Smith, *Popular Culture and Industrialism, 1865–1890* (New York: New York Univ. Press, 1967) [E168/S622] is an anthology of "beliefs and attitudes most Americans took for granted and the accepted patterns of thought and feeling after the Civil War, the stereotyped fiction, 'pseudo ideas,' and mass-produced literature" which was disseminated through the popular press. A comprehensive survey of all the popular arts has been provided by Russell B. Nye in *The Unembarrassed Muse: The Popular Arts in America* (New York: Dial, 1970) [E169/1/N92].

CHAPTER THREE
Studies in Genre

FICTION

For a complete listing of the hundreds of books and essays that critically discuss the history of American fiction, reveal its progress through one period or another, or point to a theme or method that characterizes it, the student must go to the excellent Goldentree Bibliographies on Language and Literature (see "Bibliographical Guides," p. 64 below), specifically to C. Hugh Holman, *The American Novel through Henry James* (New York: Appleton-Century-Crofts, 1966) [Z1231/F4H64] and Blake Nevius, *The American Novel: Sinclair Lewis to the Present* (New York: Appleton-Century-Crofts, 1970) [Z1231/F4N4]. For a further guide to what has been said about the American novel, see Donna Gerstenberger and George Hendrick, *The American Novel: A Checklist of Criticism of Novels Written since 1789*, 2 vols. (Denver: Swallow, 1970) (Z1231/F4G4]. Volume 1 lists criticism from 1789 to 1860; volume 2 from 1860 through 1968. Also indispensable for a listing of the thousands of novels that appeared during the first hundred years of fiction in America are Lyle H. Wright, *American Fiction, 1774–1850: A Contribution Toward a Bibliography*, 2d rev. ed. (San Marino, Calif.: Huntington Library, 1969) [Z1231/F4W9/1969] and its companion volume, *American Fiction, 1851–1875*, issued in 1957, with additions and corrections appended in 1965 (San Marino, Calif.: Huntington Library, 1965) [Z1231/F4W92/1965].

Important studies that review the development of fiction as a genre, in America and elsewhere, are Percy Lubbock, *The Craft of Fiction** (New York: Scribner's, 1921) [PN3355/L8] and E. M. Forster, *Aspects of the Novel** (New York: Harcourt, Brace, 1927) [PN3353/F6], both critical classics. Other aspects are reviewed in Melvin J. Friedman, *Stream of Consciousness: A Study in Literary Method* (New Haven: Yale Univ. Press, 1955) [PN3448/P8F7]; Leon Edel, *The Modern Psychological Novel*, rev. ed. (New York: Grosset & Dunlap, 1964) [PN3448/P8E3]; and Harry Levin, *Symbolism and Fiction* (Charlottesville: Univ. Press of Virginia, 1956) [PN3491/L4]. Georg Lukacs, *Realism in Our Time: Literature and Class Struggle** (New York: Harper & Row, 1964) [PN56/R3L793] applies Marxist interpretations to fiction. Wayne C. Booth, *The Rhetoric of Fiction** (Chicago: Univ. of Chicago Press, 1961) [PN3451/B6/1961] is highly regarded for its analysis of the ways in which narrative may be presented.

The most complete survey of the beginnings of American fiction is Henri Petter, *The Early American Novel* (Columbus: Ohio State Univ. Press, 1971) [PS375/P4]. For illuminating discussions of minor novelists before the Civil War, see Herbert Ross Brown, *The Sentimental Novel in America, 1789–1860* (Durham, N.C.: Duke Univ. Press, 1940) [PS377/B7], a delightfully written and sometimes very funny book, and Perry Miller, *The Raven and the Whale: The War of Words and Wits in the Era of Poe and Melville* (New York: Harcourt, Brace, 1956) [PS74/M5], which is also engaging, but not always to be trusted, in detail or generalization.

Important historical surveys of American fiction include Alexander
Cowie, *The Rise of the American Novel* (New York: American
Book Company, 1948) [PS371/C73], an impartial scholarly study
extending to the 1890s, and Arthur Hobson Quinn, *American Fiction: An Historical and Critical Survey* (New York, London: Appleton-Century, 1936) [PS371/Q5], which also discusses the short
story but is sometimes marred by questionable critical judgments.
Carl Van Doren, *The American Novel, 1789–1939* (New York:
Macmillan, 1940) [PS371/V3/1940], a revised edition of a 1921
publication, has largely been supplanted by the above two works,
but it is worth consulting for its astute critical opinions. All three
may be supplemented by Alfred Kazin, *On Native Grounds: An
Interpretation of American Prose Literature** (New York: Reynall
& Hitchcock, 1942) [PS379/K3] and by Kazin's equally brilliant
*Bright Book of Life: American Novelists and Storytellers from
Hemingway to Mailer** (Boston: Little, Brown, 1973) [PS379/
K25/1973].

Discriminating and sensitive insights into the continuity of themes
and motifs among nineteenth-century novelists are found in Marius
Bewley, *The Complex Fate: Hawthorne, Henry James and Some
Other American Writers* (London: Chatto & Windus, 1952)
[PS323/B4] and *The Eccentric Design: Form in the Classic Ameri-
can Novel** (New York: Columbia Univ. Press, 1959) [PS371/B4].
Everett Carter, *Howells and the Age of Realism* (Philadelphia:
Lippincott, 1954) [PS2033/C3]; Charles Child Walcutt, *American
Literary Naturalism: A Divided Stream* (Minneapolis: Univ. of
Minnesota Press, 1956) [PS379/W28]; and Donald Pizer, *Realism
and Naturalism in Nineteenth-Century American Fiction* (Carbon-
dale: Southern Illinois Univ. Press, 1960) [PS214/P5] focus on
movements during the late nineteenth century.

David W. Noble, *The Eternal Adam and the New World
Garden: The Central Myth in the American Novel since 1830**
(New York: Braziller, 1968) [PS371/N4] is an interesting but
thesis-ridden book written by a historian who argues that a central
tradition in American writing "has been the assumption that the
United States, unlike European nations, has a covenant that makes
Americans a chosen people who have escaped from the terror of
historical change to live in timeless harmony with nature." D. E. S.
Maxwell, *American Fiction: The Intellectual Background* (New

York: Columbia Univ. Press, 1963) [PS371/M3/1963] is a psychological analysis of novelists from James Fenimore Cooper to Edith Wharton, linking them to the social and political matrix in which they worked and to their British contemporaries. Daniel G. Hoffman, *Form and Fable in American Fiction* (New York: Oxford Univ. Press, 1961) [PS377/H6] traces folklore motifs in nineteenth-century novels. Harry Levin, *The Power of Blackness* (New York: Knopf, 1958) [PS1888/L4] brilliantly examines the dark brooding that underlies much mid-nineteenth-century fiction, tracing its origins partly to sources in this country, but especially to influences from abroad. This book is required reading for anyone wishing to discover moods and motifs underlying much of our best fiction of any period.

There is not yet a satisfactory survey of the achievement of American women novelists; see, however, Louis Auchincloss, *Pioneers & Caretakers: A Study of Nine American Women Novelists* (Minneapolis: Univ. of Minnesota Press, 1965) [PS151/A8/1965], a trail-breaking volume that confines itself largely to writers who have flourished in the twentieth century. Indications of activity suggest that there will soon be larger, better, and more forceful books on this subject. Anything written by Blanche H. Gelfant, Ellen Moers, or Jeanne Nostrandt will be read with interest. Annette Kolodny, *The Lay of the Land* (Chapel Hill: Univ. of North Carolina Press, 1975) [PS88/K65] explains how men have compulsively described landscape in female terms.

There is no completely adequate historical study of the short story in America. A pioneer volume is Fred Lewis Pattee, *The Development of the American Short Story: An Historical Survey* (New York and London: Harper, 1923; rpt. New York: Bilbo & Tannen, 1966) [PS374/S5P3/1966]. It is largely superseded by William Peden, *The American Short Story* (Boston: Houghton Mifflin, 1964) [PS374/S5P4], a historical and bibliographical study, and by Ray B. West, *The Short Story in America, 1900–1950* (Chicago: Regnery, 1952) [PS374/S5W4], which, though limited in scope, is a critical study that addresses itself to prevalent modes and themes that recur among twentieth-century writers of the short story. The most recent survey is Arthur Voss, *The American Short Story* (Norman: Univ. of Oklahoma Press, 1973) [PS374/S5V6].

Fiction of the twentieth century is still too much with us to allow an objectively discriminating view. There are, however, many excellent critical studies that survey the development of fiction during the past three-quarters of a century, though they sometimes tell as much about the predilections of the persons who write them as they do about the novels or novelists they discuss. Frederick J. Hoffman, *The Modern Novel, 1900–1950** (Chicago: Regnery, 1951) [PS379/H6] presents a reasoned overview of the first half century. Carl Van Doren, *Contemporary American Novelists, 1900–1920* (New York: Macmillan, 1922) [PS379/V3] contains sensitive estimates by a man who knew many of the writers of whom he wrote. Maxwell Geismar, *The Last of the Provincials: The American Novel, 1915–1925* (Boston: Houghton Mifflin, 1947) [PS379/G36] and his *Writers in Crisis: The American Novel Between Two Wars* (Boston: Houghton Mifflin, 1942) [PS379/G4], though not strictly historical, contain testy essays on eleven important novelists from Sinclair Lewis and Willa Cather to Thomas Wolfe and John Steinbeck. Frederick J. Hoffman, *The Twenties: American Writing in the Postwar Decade,** rev. ed. (New York: Collier, 1962) [PS221/H58/1962] speaks of more than fiction and is particularly valuable for its notice of social influences.

The 1930s are well reviewed by Warren French, *The Social Novel at the End of an Era* (Carbondale: Southern Illinois Univ. Press, 1966) [PS379/F68]; see also Richard Pells, *Radical Visions and American Dreams: Culture and Social Thought in the Depression Years** (New York: Harper & Row, 1973) [E379/E4], a historical survey that provides a background for Walter B. Rideout, *The Radical Novel in the United States, 1900–1954: Some Interpretations of Literature and Society** (Cambridge: Harvard Univ. Press, 1956) [PS379/R5]. The latter work begins with a backward glance into the nineteenth century, moves forward to the era of early twentieth-century muckrakers, but concentrates on writings of the 1930s and 1940s by authors who rebelled against the "human suffering imposed by some socioeconomic system" and devoted themselves as novelists to changing that system.

Marcus Klein, *After Alienation: American Novels in Mid-Century* (Cleveland and New York: World, 1964) [PS379/K5] moves forward to the 1950s, followed, though not so expertly, by Raymond M. Overman, *Beyond the Waste Land: A Study of the American*

Novel in the Nineteen-Sixties* (New Haven: Yale Univ. Press, 1972) [PS379/05]. Ihab Hassan, *Radical Innocence: Studies in the Contemporary American Novel** (Princeton: Princeton Univ. Press, 1961) [PS379/H32] employs a larger canvas to sketch the changing image of the hero in the contemporary novel as he examines "the nature of the contemporary self in action and reaction . . . sallying forth to confront experience and recoiling again to preserve its sanity or innocence." But by all odds the most informative single book on the contemporary novel is Tony Tanner, *The City of Words: American Fiction, 1950–1970* (New York: Harper & Row, 1971) [PS379/T3]. The student may safely go to it for facts as well as for ideas. Finally, another book not to be missed, and not nearly as iconoclastic as its title may suggest, is Louis D. Rubin, Jr., *The Curious Death of the Novel* (Baton Rouge: Louisiana State Univ. Press, 1967) [PS121/R78].

There are three critical studies of American fiction, written on a historical basis, that no student can do without. He may find them quirky or even beguilingly misleading; he will certainly not agree with everything they suggest, but, if his mind is open, he will not put any of them down without intellectual refreshment. The first is D. H. Lawrence, *Studies in Classic American Literature** (New York: Seltzer, 1923) [PS121/L3], often reprinted, which presents a prominent English novelist's sometimes delightfully aberrant observations on American novelists from Cooper through Melville. The second is Richard Chase, *The American Novel and Its Tradition** (Garden City: Doubleday, 1957) [PS371/C5], which argues that the American novel, when it is best and most representative, differs from the English novel because it is more romance than realistic fiction. One reason why it is romance is that, like *The Scarlet Letter, Moby-Dick, Adventures of Huckleberry Finn,* and the better novels of Henry James and William Faulkner, it suggests a great deal more than it says. The third is Leslie Fiedler, *Love and Death in the American Novel* (New York: Criterion, 1960) [PS374/L6F5], later revised and somewhat subdued (New York: Stein & Day, 1966) [PS374/L6F5/1966]. It should be read as it first appeared, a delightfully outrageous, free-swinging book, sacrilegious and sometimes impertinent, but brimming with observations and queries that command consideration. Why, for example, are there so few satisfactory females in the best American novels? Or why in so many novels is a white adolescent initiated to manhood by a dark companion? The answers suggested have seemed shocking, but they may be revealing.

DRAMA

The standard surveys of American drama are Arthur Hobson Quinn, *A History of the American Drama from the Beginning to the Civil War*, 2d ed. (New York: Crofts, 1943) [PS332/Q5/1943] and his *A History of American Drama from the Civil War to the Present Day*, rev. ed. (New York: Appleton-Century-Crofts, 1964) [PS332/Q5/1964]. Also see Joseph Wood Krutch, *The American Drama Since 1918: An Informal History*, rev. ed. (New York: Braziller, 1957) [PS351/K7/1957]. Eric Bentley, *The Playwright as Thinker* (New York: Reynal & Hitchcock, 1948) [PN1851/B4/1948] is principally concerned with European drama but contains an excellent chapter on the American theater and provides a useful introduction to trends and themes that were universally popular during the early decades of this century. John Gassner, *The Theatre in Our Times: A Survey of the Men, Materials, and Movements of the Modern Theatre* (New York: Crown, 1954) [PN1655/G3] is more broadly based and supplies more generous information on American plays and playwrights. These works can be supplemented by Gerald Weales, *American Drama Since World War II* (New York: Harcourt, Brace & World, 1962) [PS351/W4] and his *The Jumping Office: American Drama in the 1960s* (New York: Macmillan, 1969) [PS351/W43/1969]. Martin Esslin, *Theatre of the Absurd*, rev. ed. (Garden City: Doubleday, 1969) [PN1861/E8/1969], though principally concerned with European playwrights, is a popular source for information on contemporary trends. Useful collections of critical essays include Travis Bogard and William I. Oliver, eds., *Modern Drama: Essays in Criticism* (New York: Oxford Univ. Press, 1965) [PN1851/B6] and Alvin Kernan, ed., *The Modern American Theatre: A Collection of Critical Essays** (Englewood Cliffs, N.J.: Prentice-Hall, 1967) [PN2266/K38].

Other aspects of theatrical activity are reviewed by Felix Sper, *From Native Roots: A Panorama of Our Regional Drama* (Caldwell, Ind.: Caxton, 1948) [PS338/N3S6]; Robert Gard, *Grassroots*

Theater: A Search for Regional Arts in America (Madison: Univ. of Wisconsin Press, 1955) [PN2267/G3]; Cecil M. Smith, *Musical Comedy in America* (New York: Theatre Arts Books, 1950) [ML200.86]; Douglas Gilbert, *American Vaudeville: Its Life and Times* (New York: McGraw-Hill, 1940) [PN1967/G5]; Abel Green and Joe Laurie, Jr., *Show Biz: From Vaude to Video* (New York: Holt, 1951) [PN1962/G7]; Carl F. Wittke, *Tambo and Bones: A History of the American Musical Stage* (Durham, N.C.: Duke Univ. Press, 1930) [PN3195/W5]; Philip Graham, *Showboats: The History of an American Institution* (Austin: Univ. of Texas Press, 1951) [PN2293/S4G7]; and Edith J. R. Isaacs, *The Negro in the American Theatre* (New York: Theatre Arts Books, 1947) [PN2286/I8].

POETRY

Two scholarly histories of American poetry vie for acceptance as the more authoritative. The first, Roy Harvey Pearce, *The Continuity of American Poetry* (Princeton: Princeton Univ. Press, 1961) [PS303/P4], is a closely reasoned and severely critical account that discovers much poetry of our day to have derived from the influence of Walt Whitman. The second, Hyatt H. Waggoner, *American Poets from the Puritans to the Present* (Boston: Houghton Mifflin, 1968) [PS303/W3], argues the pervasive influence of Ralph Waldo Emerson on the development of American poetry. Briefer and less complete, Henry W. Wells, *The American Way of Poetry* (New York: Columbia Univ. Press, 1943) [PS303/W4] tentatively traces the gradual emergence of a distinctive American voice in poets from Philip Freneau to those prominent at the beginning of World War II. Donald Barlow Stauffer, *A Short History of American Poetry* (New York: Dutton, 1974) [PS303/S67] is more valuable for its individual essays on the poets than as a consecutive history.

Poetry in the twentieth century has often been surveyed, notably by Horace Gregory and Marya Zaturenska, *A History of American Poetry, 1900–1940* (New York: Harcourt, Brace, 1946) [PS324/G7], which has the distinction of having been written by two distinguished poets. William Van O'Connor, *Sense and Sensibility in Modern Poetry* (Chicago: Univ. of Chicago Press, 1948) [PS324/

03/1948] is rich in allusions to English-language poetry of the past as the author explains how modern poetry, through the use of myth and symbol, indirection and irony, has continued to break from the rationale of the sciences, whether pure or social, which has suggested that all things can be counted or quantified. Louise Bogan, *Achievement in American Poetry, 1900–1950** (Chicago: Regnery, 1951) [PS221/B56] is a brief but useful survey, as is Glauco Cambon, *Recent American Poetry* (Minneapolis: Univ. of Minnesota Press, 1962) [PS324/C27] and L. S. Dembo, *Conceptions of Reality in Modern American Poetry* (Berkeley: Univ. of California Press, 1966) [PS324/D45]. Longer and more discursive is Babette Deutsch, *Poetry in Our Time: A Critical Survey of Poetry in the English-Speaking World, 1900–1960,* 2d ed. (Garden City: Doubleday, 1963) [PR601/D43/1963].

The "official" history of the Imagist movement that flourished between 1914 and 1925 is Amy Lowell, *Tendencies in Modern American Poetry* (New York: Macmillan, 1917) [PS324/L8], a personal account, interesting because Miss Lowell was so ardent an advocate of that movement that Ezra Pound once suggested it should be called "Amygism." This work should be supplemented by Glen Hughes, *Imagism & the Imagists: A Study of Modern Poetry* (Stanford, Ca.: Stanford Univ. Press, 1931) [PR605/I6H8] and Stanley K. Coffman, *Imagism: A Chapter in the History of Modern Poetry* (Norman: Univ. of Oklahoma Press, 1951) [PS310/15C6], which have the added advantage of including useful bibliographies. Though Edmund Wilson's *Axel's Castle: A Study in the Imaginative Literature of 1870–1930** (New York and London: Scribner's, 1931) [PN71/W55] ranges through other literatures and genres to trace origins, tendencies, and influences from abroad, it is an indispensable reminder that poetry and what happens to it overleap national boundaries.

Critical studies of American poetry, often developed from a historical perspective, continue to recognize its transatlantic origins. Among the better of these, all the result of a burgeoning interest during the 1930s, are: R. P. Blackmur, *The Double Agent: Essays in Craft and Elucidation* (New York: Arrow, 1935) [PS324/B6], which contains some of the most sensitive and insightful observations of its time; Cleanth Brooks, *Modern Poetry and the Tradition** (Chapel Hill: Univ. of North Carolina Press, 1939) [PN1136/B75]; John Crowe

Ransom, *The World's Body** (New York: Scribner's, 1938) [PN1136/R3]; Allen Tate, *Reactionary Essays in Poetry and Ideas* (New York: Scribner's, 1936) [PN511/T3]; and Yvor Winters, *Primitivism and Decadence: A Study in American Experimental Poetry* (New York: Arrow, 1937) [PS324/W5]. This last volume, like many of the others, finds grave faults with modern experimental poetry. The fugitive movement of the 1930s is reviewed in John M. Bradbury, *The Fugitives: A Critical Account** (Chapel Hill: Univ. of North Carolina Press, 1958) [PS261/B62]; Louise Cowan, *The Fugitives: A Literary History* (Baton Rouge: Louisiana State Univ. Press, 1959) [PS261/C6]; and John L. Stewart, *The Burden of Time: The Fugitives and Agrarians* (Princeton: Princeton Univ. Press, 1965) [PS255/N357].

Later discussions that have proved useful include those in Horace Gregory, *The Shield of Achilles: Essays on Beliefs in Poetry* (New York: Current, 1949) [PN1031/R75]; Hyatt H. Waggoner, *The Heel of Elohim: Science and Values in Modern American Poetry* (Norman: Univ. of Oklahoma Press, 1950) [PS324/W3]; R. P. Blackmur, *Language as Gesture: Essays in Poetry* (New York: Harcourt, Brace, 1952) [PN1055/B55]; Murray Krieger, *The New Apologists for Poetry* (Minneapolis: Univ. of Minnesota Press, 1956) [PN1031/K7]; Stuart Holroyd, *Emergence from Chaos* (Boston: Houghton Mifflin, 1957) [PN1077/H6/1957a]; and Richard M. Ludwig, ed., *Aspects of American Poetry: Essays Presented to Howard Mumford Jones* (Columbus: Ohio State Univ. Press, 1962) [PS305/L8].

Ralph J. Mills, Jr., *Contemporary American Poetry** (New York: Random House, 1965) [PS324/M5] contains perceptive essays on some of the older poets of our time. Bruce Cook, *The Beat Generation* (New York: Scribner's, 1971) [HQ799/7/C66/1971] speaks with sympathetic understanding of poets whose life style and verse forms are often experimental. Blyden Jackson and Louis D. Rubin, Jr., *Black Poetry in America: Two Essays in Historical Interpretation* (Baton Rouge: Louisiana State Univ. Press, 1974) [PS153/N5J3] is an important pioneering attempt to measure the contribution of Afro-Americans to our total culture. It may be supplemented by James A. Emanuel and Theodore L. Gross, eds., *Dark Symphony: Negro Literature in America** (New York: Free Press, 1968) [PS508/N3E4].

Perhaps the most perceptive and reliable overview of what poets have accomplished in our time is M. L. Rosenthal, *The Modern Poets: A Critical Introduction** (New York: Oxford Univ. Press, 1960) [PR601/R6], a book in which every student may have confidence. After reading this volume, the student will want to search out other books and critical articles by Rosenthal, who has long been among the most sensitive and consistently reliable interpreters of modern verse.

Only the poets themselves speak with more authority. When in doubt about your own estimates, trust the poets when they speak of poetry. They may be opinionated, self-defensive, sometimes even argumentative, but they have been there, they know the way, and they are worth listening to. Whatever T. S. Eliot has said of poetry must be taken very seriously, as must the pronouncements of W. H. Auden, Richard Wilbur, who is particularly astute as a critic, or Randall Jarrell, who has been one of the more successful teachers of poetry in our time; see especially his *Poetry and the Age** (New York: Knopf, 1953) [PN1271/J3] and his posthumous *The Third Book of Criticism** (New York: Farrar, Straus & Giroux, 1969) [PS3519/A86A16/1969]. When faced with a choice between several anthologies of American poetry, choose first the one that has been edited by a poet; then go to the others.

Babette Deutsch, *Poetry Handbook,** 4th ed. (New York: Funk & Wagnalls, 1974) [PS44/5/D4/1974] is a comprehensive guide to the craft of poetry, including a dictionary of terms.

HUMOR

The pioneering study of homespun sources of America's literary heritage is Constance M. Rourke, *American Humor: A Study of the National Character** (New York: Harcourt, Brace, 1931) [PS430/R6]. Her posthumous *The Roots of American Culture and Other Essays** (New York: Harcourt, Brace, 1942) [E169/R/78] contains studies that were to be part of a projected history of the folk origins of native culture. That history was partially completed by Daniel G. Hoffman, *Form and Fable in American Fiction** (New York: Oxford Univ. Press, 1961) [PS377/H6]. Walter Blair, ed., *Native American Humor** (New York: American Book Company,

1937) [PN6161/B33] is a classic anthology, with an informative introduction and a useful bibliography; see also his *Horse Sense in American Humor from Benjamin Franklin to Ogden Nash* (Chicago: Univ. of Chicago Press, 1942) [PS430/B5]. Other modern collections include E. B. and Katherine S. White, eds., *A Subtreasury of American Humor** (New York: Coward-McCann, 1941) [PN6162/ W5223]; Kenneth S. Lynn, ed., *The Comic Tradition in America: An Anthology** (Garden City: Doubleday, 1958) [PS509/H8L9]; and Brom Weber, ed., *An Anthology of American Humor** (New York: Crowell, 1962) [PN6162/W42].

Richard Boyd Hauck, *A Cheerful Nihilism: Confidence and "The Absurd" in American Humorous Fiction* (Bloomington: Indiana Univ. Press, 1971) [PS430/H27] underlines what seems to its author to be an astonishing predilection among Americans to create laughter out of absurdity, even to the point of discovering a kind of beauty in the absurd. Norris Y. Yates, *The American Humorist: Conscience of the Twentieth Century** (Ames: Iowa State Univ. Press, 1964) [PS438/Y3] champions the curative power of good-natured satire, but Jesse Bier, *The Rise and Fall of American Humor* (New York: Holt, Rinehart & Winston, 1968) [PS430/B74], after a survey of humor from colonial times to the present, concludes that Americans today have lost much of their comic sense to disillusionment and despair. Bier's view is not entirely shared in Louis D. Rubin, Jr., ed., *The Comic Imagination in American Literature* (New Brunswick, N.J.: Rutgers Univ. Press, 1973) [PS430/R8], in which twenty-five scholars in thirty-one essays mine lodes of humor from John Smith to Joseph Heller and John Barth, demonstrating how American comic writing from colonial times to the present has been nourished by the conflict between the way in which many people naturally speak and act—which is colloquially and perhaps vulgarly —and the way other people think they *should* speak and act—in cultured language and politely; it is the friction between these two tendencies that has excited the risibility of most Americans.

Recently, an American Humor Studies Association has been established; the group sponsors *American Humor: An Interdisciplinary Newsletter,* which is published at Virginia Commonwealth University and the University of Maryland, and a journal, *Studies in American Humor,* published at Southwest Texas State University.

CHAPTER FOUR

Foreign Influences and Influence Abroad

ᛦ ᛦ ᛦ American literature has long been nurtured by literatures from abroad, but, from the time of Benjamin Franklin to the present, it has also influenced other literatures. Influences from abroad are examined in Howard Mumford Jones, *America and French Culture, 1750–1848* (Chapel Hill: Univ. of North Carolina Press, 1927) [E1838/F8J7]; Stanley T. Williams, *The Spanish Backgrounds of American Literature*, 2 vols. (New Haven: Yale Univ. Press, 1955) [PS159/S7W5]; and Henry A. Pochmann, *German Culture in America: Philosophical and Literary Influences, 1600–1900* (Madison: Univ. of Wisconsin Press, 1950) [PS157/D4], each a monument of modern literary scholarship. Margaret

Denny and William H. Gilman, eds., *The American Writer and the European Tradition* (Minneapolis: Univ. of Minnesota Press, 1950) [PS157/04] contains essays by several prominent scholars on how native writers have responded to transatlantic influences. Lawrence W. Chisolm, *Fenollosa: The Far East and American Culture* (New Haven: Yale Univ. Press, 1963) [N8375/F375/C5] explains how, through the influence of anthropologist Ernest Fenollosa, the lore and literary forms of the Far East have found they way into modern American literature; for earlier influences, see Arthur E. Christy, *The Orient in American Transcendentalism* (New York: Columbia Univ. Press, 1932) [B905/C5].

The impact of American culture abroad is discussed in Halvdan Koht, *The American Spirit in Europe: A Survey of Transatlantic Influences* (Philadelphia: Univ. of Pennsylvania Press, 1949) [E1837/K64] and Bertrand Russell and others, *The Impact of America on European Culture* (Boston: Beacon, 1954) [CB425/I43]. Henry Steele Commager, ed., *America in Perspective: The United States through Foreign Eyes* (New York: Random House, 1947) [E1691/C67] and Allen Nevins, ed., *America through British Eyes*, rev. ed. (New York: Oxford Univ. Press, 1948) [E169/1/N52/1948] are collections of statements about America, including its literature, made by Europeans over a hundred-year period.

William B. Cairns, *British Criticisms of American Writings, 1783–1815: A Contribution to the Study of Anglo-American Literary Relationships* (Madison: Univ. of Wisconsin Press, 1948) [PN35/W65/No. 1] is extended by Clarence Gohdes, *American Literature in Nineteenth-Century England* (New York: Columbia Univ. Press, 1944) [PS159/G8G6]. Further studies of early influences of nineteenth-century American literature abroad are needed; they can be modeled after Paul C. Weber, *America in German Literature in the First Half of the Nineteenth Century* (New York: Columbia Univ. Press, 1926) [PT149/A5W4/1926a] and Gilbert H. Fess, *The American Revolution in Creative French Literature, 1775–1939* (Columbia: Univ. of Missouri Studies, 1941) [PQ1457/A5/F4].

More recent influences have been more fully investigated in Thelma M. Smith and Ward L. Miner, *Transatlantic Migration: The Contemporary American Novel in France* (Durham, N.C.: Duke Univ. Press, 1955) [PS161/F7S6]; Anne M. Springer, *The*

American Novel in Germany: A Study of the Critical Reception of American Novelists between the Two World Wars (Hamburg: Cram, De Gruyter, 1960) [PS159/G3S6]; Donald W. Heiney, *America in Modern Italian Literature* (New Brunswick, N.J.: Rutgers Univ. Press, 1964) [PQ4054/A5H4]; Carl L. Anderson, *The Swedish Acceptance of American Literature* (Philadelphia: Univ. of Pennsylvania Press, 1957) [PS161/S9A5]; Deming B. Brown, *Soviet Attitudes toward American Writing* (Princeton: Princeton Univ. Press, 1962) [PS159/R8B7]; and C. D. Narasimhaiah, ed., *Asian Response to American Literature* (Delhi: Vikas, 1972) [PA7/A8]. Sigmund Skard, *American Studies in Europe: Their History and Present Organization,* 2 vols. (Philadelphia: Univ. of Pennsylvania Press, 1958) [E1758/S65] presents a historical survey of courses in American literature or culture in European universities.

CHAPTER FIVE
Language

❦ ❦ ❦ To make a study of language interesting, even amusing, to the general reader was the massive but lighthearted accomplishment of H. L. Mencken, *The American Language: An Inquiry into the Development of English in the United States*, 4th ed. (New York: Knopf, 1945) [PE2808/M43] and its two giant and equally readable supplements in 1945 and 1948. George Philip Krapp, *The English Language in America*, 2 vols. (New York: Century, 1925) [PE2808/K7] is scholarly and still authoritative, but it emphasizes pronunciation more than it does vocabulary. It·is extended but not supplanted by M. M. Mathews, ed., *The Beginnings of American English: Essays and Comments* (Chicago: Univ. of Chicago Press, 1931)

[PE2805/M3]; Thomas Pyles, *Words and Ways of American English* (New York: Random House, 1952) [PE2808/P9]; Albert H. Marckwardt, *American English* (New York: Oxford Univ. Press, 1958) [PE2808/M3]; and Carlton Laird, *Language in America* (New York: World, 1970) [PE2808/L3], perhaps the most simple and useful of these volumes.

Sir William Craigie and James P. Hurlbert, eds., *A Dictionary of American English on Historical Principles*, 4 vols. (Chicago: Univ. of Chicago Press, 1938–1944) [PE2835/C72] is a standard work in the field. M. M. Mathews, *A Dictionary of Americanisms on Historical Principles*, 2 vols. (Chicago: Univ. of Chicago Press, 1951) [PE2835/D5] stresses contributions made by Americans to the English language. American slang is recorded in Maurice H. Weseen, *A Dictionary of American Slang* (New York: Crowell, 1934) [PE3729/A5W4]; Harold Wentworth and Stuart B. Flexner, *Dictionary of American Slang* (New York: Crowell, 1967) [PE3729/U5W4/1966]; and Eric Partridge, *A Dictionary of Slang and Unconventional English*, 7th ed. (New York: Macmillan, 1970) [PE3721/P322]. Hyman E. Golden and others, *Dictionary of American Underworld Lingo* (New York: Twayne, 1950) [PE3726/D5] is not only informative but amusing. J. L. Dillard, *A History of the English Language in America* (New York: Random House, 1975) [PE2808/D6] demonstrates how African dialects, sailors' slang, traders' lingua franca, and American Indian dialects all have had a major influence on the development of language in this country; Dillard's *Black English: Its History and Usage in the United States* (New York: Random House, 1972) [PE3102/N4/D5] is an important pioneer study.

CHAPTER SIX
Types and Schools of Criticism

❦ ❦ ❦ Criticism is a toothsome dish which can be divided in many ways into many attractive portions. There are perhaps as many critical approaches to literature as there are critics who examine it. And it is not an unusual characteristic of the critical mind that each critic should consider his approach to be the best. The one who does is called an *absolutist critic;* the one who keeps an open mind, acknowledging the usefulness of various, even contradictory, approaches, is called a *relativistic critic.* He becomes involved in *theoretical criticism* when he looks for general principles that certify excellence in literature or in one of its genres, or he may think of himself as a *practical critic* who tests principles against the actualities presented by particular writings.

The most ancient and most tenacious quarrel among critics is that between the critics who hold, with Plato, that literature must be useful and those who simplify Aristotle into seeming to say that it must please. In America, until recently and with few noteworthy voices raised in opposition except that of Edgar Allan Poe, usefulness has been required. It has been suggested, however, that there are four basic categories into which all literary criticism falls. Attention may be focused on (1) the work itself as an artifact with recognizable structural characteristics; (2) the maker of that work—why he did what he did, what he intended; (3) the relationship between the work and the universe that it pretends to reproduce; and (4) the effect of the work on readers, the instruction or pleasure it gives, the good it produces.

The oldest of these types of criticism is the third, called the *mimetic approach*. It views art, including literature, as an imitation of aspects of the universe, of external and immutable ideas, of eternal and unchanging patterns of sound, sight, movement, or form. The type of criticism most widely heard in the Western world, however, has been the fourth, called the *pragmatic approach*, which evaluates a literary work in terms of its usefulness as instruction, entertainment, or emotional stimulation. When attention focuses on the writer himself, his imagination, insight, or spontaneity, that is the *expressive approach*. The first type of criticism, the *objective approach*, made popular in our time by the "New Criticism" (see pp. 54–55, below) that gained influence in the 1930s, attempts to isolate the work of art from the other three external points of view, to see it as an autonomous object, a self-contained entity, a thing in itself with a life and structure of its own.

The *reasons* why critics criticize may be as various as the critics themselves. A particular critic may wish to justify himself or his methods, as Edgar Allan Poe does in "The Philosophy of Composition," as Henry James does in the introductions written late in life to the New York edition of his works, or as William Faulkner seems to have done in his speech of acceptance of the Nobel Prize in literature. He may wish simply to instruct, as the new critics or most college teachers do, by pointing to outstanding passages, characterizations, or patterns. He may wish to apply rules or defend aesthetic principles. Confident of his own expertise, he may wish to guide or legislate taste. Or he may be an adherent of any number of critical approaches, now relying on one, now on another, for critics can be as mercurial and elusive as literature itself.

In America, what literary criticism existed in the seventeenth century had a utilitarian and religious orientation; it looked for plainness in writing, which was supposed to instruct or correct: "God's altar," said the Puritan clergyman-writer John Cotton, "needs no polishing." In the eighteenth century, criticism tended to be conservative and neoclassic, finding ideals of order, restraint, good taste, and decorum in the writings of Homer, Virgil, Horace. That literature was most admired which pleased by its proportions at the same time that it instructed or corrected man, usually in his relations with other men. Alexander Pope, Jonathan Swift, and the English periodical essayists provided contemporary models worthy of American imitation. In the early nineteenth century, elements of romanticism were introduced, deriving from attitudes championed by William Wordsworth and Samuel Taylor Coleridge in England, Jean Jacques Rousseau in France, and such German philosophers as Immanuel Kant and Johann Gottlieb Fichte.

Many attempts have been made to define romanticism, but so various are its guises that it has been suggested that the word always be used in the plural, that is, that critics should speak of "romanticisms" rather than of "romanticism." One clearly identifiable characteristic of the romantic of the nineteenth or any other century is his individualism. He is likely to look into his own heart to write, secure in his reliance on what he finds there because it is an expression of his own "self." He might believe, as Edgar Allan Poe did, in values of craftsmanship and feel that, at its best, literature bears no relation to morality; he might believe with Ralph Waldo Emerson that art serves moral ends and that its form is organic, so that each subject seeks its own natural form; or with Walt Whitman, he might simply sing himself and celebrate himself, assuming that what is true for him is true for all men. Like Walter Scott in England and James Fenimore Cooper and William Gilmore Simms in this country, he might find measures of individual achievement in tales of adventure laid in the past. He might plumb, as Poe did, the regions of terror and horror that haunt the human mind.

After the Civil War, realism was in the ascendancy, spurred on by such powerful spokesmen as William Dean Howells and Henry James. Writers were encouraged to look about them, to portray native scenes and set forth recognizable native notions of decorum or morality, to observe and record the reactions of characteristically American people as they were confronted with familiar or unfamiliar social situations at home or abroad. By the end of the nineteenth century, many critics had begun to recognize among American writers a naturalism, similar to that of Emile Zola in France, in which humankind was likely to be viewed as a species of animal buffeted by internal drives and external forces quite beyond its control. Then, as the twentieth century advanced, students of native literature began to search for its roots in the American past, finding the literature more often an expression of American cultural values than an entity in itself. Soon literary historians and critics of various persuasions were lined in battle, defending a multitude of attitudes.

An excellent survey of criticism in general is William K. Wimsatt, Jr., and Cleanth Brooks, *Literary Criticism: A Short History* (New York: Knopf, 1957) [PN86/W5]. For definitions of critical terms, C. Hugh Holman, *A Handbook to Literature,** 3rd ed. (Indianapolis: Odyssey, 1972) [PN41/H6/1972] is indispensable. For criticism in America, see George E. DeMille, *Literary Criticism in America: A Preliminary Survey* (New York: Dial, 1931) [PS62/D41]; William Charvat, *The Origins of American Critical Thought, 1810–1835** (Philadelphia: Univ. of Pennsylvania Press, 1936) [PS74/C45]; the collaborative study edited for the American Literature Group of the Modern Language Association of America by Floyd Stovall, *The Development of American Literary Criticism** (Chapel Hill: Univ. of North Carolina Press, 1955) [PN99/U5S75]; John Paul Pritchard, *Criticism in America* (Norman: Univ. of Oklahoma Press, 1956) [PN99/U5P69], which surveys critical theory from the late eighteenth century to the middle of the nineteenth century; and Benjamin Spencer, *The Quest for Nationality: An American Literary Campaign* (Syracuse: Syracuse Univ. Press, 1957) [PS88/S58], which measures criticism against other changing patterns of American culture.

Attitudes of leading American critics of the first half of the twentieth century are analyzed in Stanley Edgar Hyman, *The Armed Vision: A Study in the Methods of Modern Literary Criti-*

cism* (New York: Knopf, 1952) [PN94/H9] and Walter Sutton, *Modern American Criticism* (Englewood Cliffs, N.J.: Prentice-Hall, 1963) [PN99/U5S8]. Excellent anthologies are Morton Dauwen Zabel, ed., *Literary Opinion in America: Essays Illustrating the Status, Methods, and Problems of Criticism in the United States in the Twentieth Century*, rev. ed. (New York: Harper, 1951) [PN771/Z2] and Clarence Arthur Brown, *The Achievement of American Criticism: Representative Selections from Three Hundred Years of American Criticism* (New York: Ronald, 1954) [PN99/U5B7].

As has been suggested here, the attractive occupation called criticism can be divided into just about as many parts as there are critics who engage in it: there is *Formal Criticism*, which examines a work of art in terms of the requirements of the type or genre to which it belongs; *judicial criticism*, which applies authoritative standards, often derived from Aristotle (for years there was a rigorous school of Aristotelian criticism at the University of Chicago), or other objective criteria to analyze, classify, define, or evaluate works of art; and *theoretical criticism*, which attempts to discover general principles that govern literature at its best and to formulate inclusive and enduring aesthetic and critical tenets. But these divisions so impose on and overlap one another that, it has been said, they cause a student's head to ache on one side. When the hapless student learns that, in opposition to these, there is something called *practical criticism* (also sometimes called *applied criticism*), a popular do-it-yourself variety in which the critic's own principles of art and aesthetic beliefs, usually derived from one of the kinds of criticism mentioned above, are applied to specific works of art, his head may begin to ache on the other side.

The kinds of criticism identified below are those most often used today; therefore, differentiations among them are most useful to the student. Tomorrow may tell—in fact, inevitably will tell—another story.

BIOGRAPHICAL CRITICISM

The French critic Charles Augustin Sainte-Beuve (1804–1869) once wrote, "There are in poetry no good and bad subjects; there are only good and bad poets." From statements such as this there has arisen a kind of criticism with various emphases. First, it can assume that the investigation of the life of an artist can somehow illuminate problematic aspects of his writings, such as ironies or the author's stands on issues, which, without biographical information, would remain unclear. Next, since all literature need not be problematic, biographical materials can be used to intensify the effect of a literary work by explaining the context of its creation and the forces impinging on the author's life which promoted or obstructed its completion. Finally, the work of literature can be studied, not as an end in itself, but as a means for examining and explaining the nature of the creative process, the idiosyncrasies or predilections of the author, or the literary personality in general. Biographical critics are sometimes likely to overemphasize the importance of incidents in a writer's life and find them obsessively repeated in his writings, not always recognizing that, while this may be the case in some instances, it is not necessarily the case in all. (See "Psychological Criticism," below.)

EXISTENTIALIST CRITICISM

Existentialism is a view of the world, made popular during the late nineteenth and the early twentieth centuries, that centers on the uniqueness and the isolation of individual experience in a universe that is indifferent or even hostile. The fact of existence, even of the existence of man, is thought to be impossible to explain; but people nonetheless somehow mysteriously do, or can, control their destiny through freedom of choice, so that ultimately every person must accept responsibility for whatever he or she does. At the same time, however, a sense of the meaninglessness and absurdity of the world, and of a person's existence or actions, produces anxiety (*angst*). To many existentialists, the person is alienated from, at the same time that he is captive within, a world that is completely absurd (cannot be rationally explained), a circumstance that releases him of responsibility to anything but the lonely absurdity of his own existence. To others, the person quietly does the best he can, alone or in cooperation with others, to live decently within a world governed by incomprehensible forces that are accepted with awe or even reverence. Within such a framework, however, so many variations have appeared, especially when a literary work or a writer is the subject of scrutiny, that a precise or comprehensive definition that will satisfy all existentialists is probably impossible. It has even been said that one characteristic of the existentialist critic is his bemused lack of intellectual precision. Sidney Finkelstein, *Existentialism and Alienation in American Literature* (New York: International, 1960) [PS78/F7] explains the origins of existentialism in Europe and its application in recent literature in the United States.

FREUDIAN CRITICISM

Sigmund Freud (1856–1939) described the creative impulse as deriving from hidden springs of motivation in the unconscious of (1) the *id*, which is in the unconscious mind and is associated with instinctual impulses and demands for immediate satisfaction of primitive needs, (2) the *ego*, which is conscious and acts as a mediator between the requirements of the id for primitive satisfaction, and (3) the *superego*, which is a kind of censor or conscience that develops through perception of moral standards of the community. Freud often stripped literary situations to basic levels, such as that of the *libido*—the psychic, emotional energy associated with instinctive biological drives, usually sexual. These drives often produced an Oedipal situation where an unconscious love for the mother and hatred and jealousy of the father became sources of conflict. He discovered that the basis for a great deal of literature was the conflict between the security provided by the mother, even in the womb, and the masculine (phallic) forces of energy, conquest, and often destruction. For a study of the effects of Freud on literature, see Frederick J. Hoffman, *Freudianism and the Literary Mind** (Baton Rouge: Louisiana State Univ. Press, 1957) [PN49/H6/1957].

HISTORICAL CRITICISM

The French critic and historian Hippolyte Taine (1828–1893) held that a literary work might be most profitably studied in relation

to what he called race, milieu, and time—as "a transcript of contemporary manners, a manifestation of a certain kind of mind." The
historical critic examines a literary work in terms of the social and
historical context in which it was produced and is less concerned
with explaining the meaning of the work for his or her own time
than with demonstrating the meaning of the work for the people
in the time and place in which it was written. Such an approach
can point to shifts in taste from one generation to another. It can
also search out those elements of a literary work that make it, or
do not make it, immortal. For a defense of the historical method, see
Robert E. Spiller, "Literary History," in *The Aims and Methods of
Scholarship in Modern Languages and Literatures,** ed. James Thorp
(New York: Modern Language Association of America, 1970)
[PB22/T7/1970].

IMPRESSIONISTIC CRITICISM

"I like what I like because I like it" has been, perhaps from time
immemorial, a popular response to literature. The critic who espouses
it is said to be an impressionist. He can cross the boundaries of any
other critical persuasion, extracting what he likes or finds interesting; his only requirement of literature is that it must somehow
move or impress. A rich, open, personal response to literature is
encouraged, and all personal experience and extraneous linkings
are considered to be valid aims in the cultivation of a reaction to
what is read. "Use any means, but get people to like it." One of the
least sophisticated methods of criticism, it nonetheless has a kind
of contagion value and is often used as a pedagogical tool to encourage a vital and direct experience of literature.

MARXIST CRITICISM

Deriving from the political and economic philosophy of Karl
Marx (1818–1883) and Friedrich Engels (1820–1895) and especially influential in this country in the writing and criticism of fiction
in the 1930s, Marxist criticism is based on an adaptation of the
dialectical doctrine set forth by the German philosopher George
Wilhelm Friedrich Hegel (1770–1831). This doctrine explains that
things as they are (*thesis*) are continually confronted by forces of

change (*antithesis*), out of which conflict comes a new state (*synthesis*) that stabilizes to a new thesis, which requires a new antithesis, and so on. What the Marxist critic calls dialectical realism is an interpretation of reality that views matter as the sole subject of change and all change as the product of a constant conflict between opposites arising from internal contradictions inherent in all things. Human history, and especially class struggle, is viewed as a natural evolutionary process in constant flux. When a Marxist critic speaks of "social realism," he or she is likely to be referring, not to life as it is, but to life as it could or should be as a result of evolutionary or revolutionary change. He or she may believe that a writer who identifies with mistreated people, usually designated "the proletariat," comes closer to truth than the writer who submits to aesthetic or spiritual notions that cloud his or her perception of the tensions among social forces. But the Marxist critic need not be, in a political sense, an advocate of communism or revolution by force. When conflicts with society are revealed by the novelist, playwright, or poet, those revelations themselves may become instruments of social change. For a study of this theme in its application to fiction see Georg Lukacs, *Realism in Our Time: Literature and the Class Struggle** (New York: Harper & Row, 1964) [PN56/R3L793].

MYTHIC CRITICISM

Carl Jung (1875–1961) was a disciple of Sigmund Freud (see "Freudian Criticism"), and his theory of mythical motifs is not unrelated to Freud's search for conflicts in literature that reflect universal needs and fears. Myth critics search for patterns of imagery and symbolism, especially of regeneration and rebirth, that recur again and again in the literatures of many lands. Their search is for the mythic core that is concealed by the web of artistic structure. Jung explained the recurrence of such myths as the result of a "collective unconscious," a sublimated racial memory that each generation passes on to the next; but modern writers such as T. S. Eliot, William Faulkner, and John Updike seem intentionally to have recreated myths for modern readers. Sir James George Frazer, (1854–1941) in *The Golden Bough*, 3rd ed. (New York: Macmillan, 1935) [BL310/F7/1935], traces cycles of myths that recur in the literatures of many cultures. Northrop Frye, in his *Anatomy of Criticism* (Princeton: Princeton Univ. Press, 1957) [PN81/F75], suggests correspondences between such genres as comedy, romance, tragedy, and satire and the seasons of the year: spring, summer, fall, and winter. Like Havelock Ellis (1859–1939) in *The Dance of Life* (Boston and New York: Houghton Mifflin, 1923) [PR6009/L8D3/1923a], he discovers rhythms in nature that parallel rhythms in art. For a brief discussion, see Wallace W. Douglas, "The Meaning of 'Myth' in Modern Criticism," *Modern Philology*, 50 (May 1953), 232–42 or Northrop Frye, "Literature and Myth," in *The Relations of Literary Study: Essays on Interdisciplinary Contributions**, ed. James Thorp (New York: Modern Language Association of America, 1967) [PN519/T14].

NEW CRITICISM

In the 1920s many critics began to revolt against discussing literature in historical, biographical, mythic, or even ethical terms. Instead, they would concentrate attention on the work itself, its tone and texture, its internal tensions, and its imagery, word patterns, and unique symbolism. Each work of literature was autonomous, a thing in itself, to be judged for itself and not in relation to anything outside itself. Influential in establishing this view were such early essays of Ezra Pound as "Instigations" (1920) and "How to Read" (1931), which may be most conveniently found in Ezra Pound, *The Literary Essays*, edited with an introduction by T. S. Eliot (London: Faber and Faber, 1954) [PN511/P625a/1954a]. Other influential sources have been Eliot's own *The Sacred Wood: Essays on Poetry and Criticism* (London: Methuen, 1920) [PN511/E44/1920]; I. A. Richard's *Practical Criticism: A Study of Literary Judgment* (London: Paul, Trench, Truber, 1929) [PN1031/R48]; Edith Rickert, *New Methods for the Study of Literature* (Chicago: Univ. of Chicago Press, 1927) [PN175/R5]; and the popular textbooks by Cleanth Brooks and Robert Penn Warren, *Understanding Poetry*, 2d ed. (New York: Appleton-Century-Crofts, 1959) [PN3335/B7/1959] and *Understanding Fiction*, 3rd ed. (New York: Holt, Rinehart & Winston, 1960) [PR1109/B676/1960].

Because it required an independent reading of literature by critics of often divergent backgrounds, training, or intellectual attitudes, the New Criticism in the 1930s and later often developed in diverse directions, but it has nonetheless been responsible for some of the most acute critical observations of our century, set forth in volumes that are still read with interest—though not always with complete approval. A liberal education in modern literary criticism can be obtained by reading, in addition to the books mentioned above, the following diverse but almost equally influential works: R. P. Blackmur, *The Double Agent* (New York: Arrow, 1935) [PS324/B6]; *The Expense of Greatness* (New York: Arrow, 1940) [PR473/B56]; *Language as Gesture: Essays in Poetry* (New York: Harcourt, Brace, 1950) [PN1055/B55]; *The Lion and the Honeycomb: Essays in Solicitude and Critique* (New York: Harcourt, Brace, 1955) [PS121/B59]; Cleanth Brooks, *The Well Wrought Urn: Studies in the Structure of Poetry* (New York: Harcourt, Brace, 1947) [PR502/B7]; Kenneth Burke, *The Philosophy of Literary Form: Studies in Symbolic Action,* 2d ed. (Baton Rouge: Louisiana State Univ. Press, 1967) [PN511/B795/1967]; Francis Fergusson, *The Idea of a Theatre: A Study of Ten Plays; The Art of Drama in Changing Perspective* (Princeton: Princeton Univ. Press, 1949) [PN1661/F4]; John Crowe Ransom, *God Without Thunder: An Unorthodox Defense of Orthodoxy* (New York: Harcourt, Brace, 1930) [BL240/R25]; Ransom's *The World's Body* (New York: Scribner's, 1938) [PN1136/R3]; and his *The New Criticism* (Norfolk, Conn.: New Directions, 1941) [PN1031/R3]; Allen Tate, *Reactionary Essays in Poetry and Ideas* (New York: Scribner's, 1936) [PN511/T3]; *Reason In Madness* (New York: Putnam's, 1941) [PN511/T33]; *The Forlorn Demon* (Chicago: Regnery, 1953) [PN37/T28]; and Yvor Winters, *Primitivism and Decadence* (1937) and *Maule's Curse* (1938), both of which are reprinted in his *In Defense of Reason* (New York: Swallow, 1947) [PS121/W53].

An excellent critique of these and other New Critics will be found in Richard Foster, *The New Romantics: A Reappraisal of the New Criticism* (Bloomington: Indiana Univ. Press, 1962) [PN94/F6]. Collections of selected essays by many of the New Critics include R. W. Stallman, ed., *The Critic's Notebook* (Minneapolis: Univ. of Minnesota Press, 1950) [PN81/S66] and Ray B. West, Jr., ed., *Essays on Modern Literary Criticism* (New York: Rinehart, 1952) [PN85/W4].

NEW HUMANISM

A brief but intense movement of the 1920s and 1930s rejected both what it considered the extravagances of romanticism, which viewed man as he would like to be, and the grimness of realism, which in its naturalistic form portrayed man as an animal urged on by gigantic forces beyond his control; instead, the followers of this movement viewed man as a being endowed with a power of will that allowed him to control himself and, to some extent, direct the course of his ethical and moral development. The movement was influenced by Irving Babbitt, who advocated recognition of an "inner principle of restraint" in *Literature and the American College: Essays in Defense of Humanism* (Boston and New York: Houghton Mifflin, 1908) [LC1011/B2], and who continued that advocacy in: *The New Laokoon: An Essay on the Confusion of the Arts* (Boston and New York: Houghton Mifflin, 1910) [N66/B2]; *Rousseau and Romanticism* (Boston and New York: Houghton Mifflin, 1919) [PN603/B3]; and *Democracy and Leadership* (Boston and New York: Houghton Mifflin, 1924) [SC423/B18].

The movement was also influenced by Paul Elmer More, whose meticulously written, multivolumed *Shelburne Essays* (New York: Putnam, 1904–1921) [PR99/M7] and *New Shelburne Essays* (Princeton: Princeton Univ. Press, 1928–1936) [PN511/M48] were widely admired. Encouraged by T. S. Eliot and led by Norman Foerster, the New Humanists in 1930 published a provocative symposium, *Humanism and America: Essays on the Outlook of Modern Civilization* (New York: Farrar and Rinehart, 1930) [B821/F6], which called forth severe and chiding responses from advocates of the New Criticism (see above). C. Hartley Grattan edited an answering symposium, *The Critique of Humanism* (New York: Brewer and Warren, 1930) [B821/G7], and George Santayana attacked the humanists in *The Genteel Tradition at Bay* (New York: Scribner's, 1931) [B821/S17].

PHENOMENOLOGICAL CRITICISM

Deriving from theories set forth early in this century by the German philosopher Edmund Husserl, phenomenology has long been popular in Europe and is now making important inroads in this country. Most simply stated, it is a descriptive philosophy of experience and of the objects of experience. Its advocates take a fresh hard look at phenomena themselves without prejudgment or the intrusion of dogma. They claim to see the world as if for the first time, describing it exactly as it is, or as it seems to be to them. Because the philosophy depends on individual observation, it may tend to become subjective, in some of its aspects not unlike American transcendentalism of the nineteenth century. Because it is somewhat subjective, it has taken many directions, as a method of cognition rather than as an organized school. Perhaps the best introduction to it is Martin Farber, *The Aims of Phenomenology: The Motives, Methods, and Impact of Husserl's Thought* (New York: Harper & Row, 1966) [B3279/H94F29]. To see the method applied to a work of American literature, see Paul Brodtkorb, *Ishmael's White World: A Phenomenological Reading of Moby-Dick* (New Haven: Yale Univ. Press, 1965) [PS2384/M62B7].

PSYCHOLOGICAL CRITICISM

When principles of modern psychology (see "Freudian Criticism" and "Mythic Criticism," above) are applied by critics either to characters or situations within a work of literature or to the person who wrote that work, the resultant criticism is said to be psychological or psychoanalytical. But the term has been so widely used, and misused, that it is perhaps better to avoid it. Putting an author or a character on the psychoanalyst's couch may seem to be taking unfair advantage of that person, who is not really there to describe or defend himself, but it is an occupation that many critics enjoy and that sometimes produces provocative insights; see, for example, Marie Bonaparte, *The Life and Works of Edgar Allan Poe: A Psycho-Analytical Interpretation* (London: Imago, 1949) [PS2631/B62]. An excellent discussion of what has been done, correctly and incorrectly, in applying psychoanalytical principles is Louis Fraiberg, *Psychoanalysis & American Literary Criticism* (Detroit: Wayne State Univ. Press, 1960) [PS78/F7].

STRUCTURALIST CRITICISM

To avoid the confusion of attitudes loosely suggested by existential-ism and Marxism, structuralism has been proposed, not as an ideology, but as a method of looking at literature that has ideological implica-tions. Its intention is to be precise. Therefore, it takes its start from modern linguistics, which is often based on mathematical formula-tions that measure the manner in which an author manages his linguistic possibilities—that is, how he orders his words, sentences, and paragraphs into a coherent, or incoherent, whole. By moving from the study of language to the study of literature, which is language massed toward meaning, structuralism seeks to discover principles of structure that certify or reject a particular piece of literature as a work of art. Robert Scholes, *Structuralism in Litera-ture: An Introduction* (New Haven: Yale Univ. Press, 1974) [PN98/S753], p. 10, explains, "At the heart of structuralism is the idea of system: a complete, self-regulating entity that adapts to new conditions by transforming its features while retaining its systematic structure. In particular, we can look at individual works, literary genres, and the whole of literature as related systems, and at literature as a system within the larger system of human culture." The attempt to apply the precision of science—if, indeed, in its highest reaches science is really precise—to humanistic activities is not a new endeavor; social scientists have often suggested that a person's morals and art might submit to quantitative measurement. Now, secure in the belief that man is part of and exists within an orderly and intelligible system, and aided by the ingenuities of computers, which can search that system out, structuralists may reveal interesting and factual evidence of, among other things, writers and writing. People who consider structuralism an attractive, fashionable, will-of-the-wisp pursuit are likely to be considered old-fashioned; other people, however skeptical, watch the development of it with interest, and wish it well.

TEXTUAL CRITICISM

Recognizing that criticism of a text that is not presented in exactly the form in which its author intended it to appear, can only result in distorted appraisals, scholars for the past several years have been attempting to reconstruct the texts of American authors according to precise principles set down by The Center for Editions of American Authors, which is sponsored by the Modern Language Association of America; see *Statement of Editorial Principles and Procedures: A Working Manual for Editing Nineteenth-Century American Texts*, rev. ed. (New York: Modern Language Association of America, 1972) [PN162/M6/1972]. Manuscript sources are sought out to determine whether an author's text has been tampered with by editors or typesetters; galley proofs, when available, are examined to determine what deviations from the manuscript were authorial; changes in later editions or reprintings of a text are examined and evidence is sought to determine whether these had been approved by the author. The textual critic attempts to be completely objective. He uses whatever knowledge is available to him in the areas of literary history and biographical detail—especially material about the work habits of the author, including such things as his idiosyncrasies in penmanship and punctuation; the critic must know publishing history and the personal peculiarities of publishers, editors, and compositors who do or do not apply their own systems of punctuation, spelling, or capitalization when setting an author's manuscript in type. Textual criticism often involves such tedious and painstaking attention to detail that it has been suggested that it is not criticism at all, but textual scholarship. Its advocates, however, find no distinction between criticism and scholarship, insisting that their findings result in literary criticism of the highest order, and they are probably right. For guides that will lead to other guides, see the essays, notably those by Fredson Bowers and William B. Todd, in *Bibliography and Textual Criticism*, ed. O. M. Brack, Jr., and Warner Barnes (Chicago: Univ. of Chicago Press, 1969) [Z2011/B733] and in *Art and Error: Modern Textual Editing*, ed. Ronald Gottesman and Scott Bennett (Bloomington: Indiana Univ. Press, 1970) [PN162/G63]; see also James Thorpe, *Principles of Textual Criticism* (San Marino, Ca.: The Huntington Library, 1972) [PR65/T5].

CHAPTER SEVEN
Periodicals

❦ ❦ ❦ The standard authorities on the publication of periodicals in America are Frank Luther Mott, *A History of American Magazines,* 5 vols. (Cambridge: Harvard Univ. Press, 1938–1968) [PN4877/M63/1938]; Frederick J. Hoffman, Charles Allen, and Carolyn F. Ulrich, *The Little Magazine: A History and Bibliography,* 2d ed. (Princeton: Princeton Univ. Press, 1947) [PN4836/H6/1947]; and Frank Luther Mott, *American Journalism: A History, 1690–1930,* 3rd ed. (New York: Macmillan, 1962) [PN4855/M63/1962].

Listed below are periodicals of particular value for the student of American literature, each preceded by the abbreviation by which it is customarily designated and followed by the place of its publication, its publisher or sponsor, and the year in which it first appeared.

AAS   *Abstracts of English Studies.* Champaign, Ill.: National Council of Teachers of English, 1958.

AL   *American Literature: A Journal of Literary History, Criticism, and Bibliography.* Durham, N.C.: Duke Univ. Press, 1928.

ALA   *American Literature Abstracts.* Stockton, Ca., 1967.

ALR   *American Literary Realism, 1870–1910.* Arlington: Univ. of Texas, 1967.

AN&Q   *American Notes and Queries.* New Haven: American Notes & Queries, 1902.

AQ   *American Quarterly.* Philadelphia: Univ. of Pennsylvania, 1951.

ATQ   *American Transcendental Quarterly.* Hartford, Conn.: The Emerson Society, 1969.

BMMLA   *Bulletin of the Midwest Modern Language Association.* Iowa City: Univ. of Iowa, 1968.

BRMMLA   *Bulletin of the Rocky Mountain Modern Language Association.* Boulder: Univ. of Colorado, 1968.

CLAJ   *CLA Journal.* Baltimore: College Language Association, 1957.

CE   *College English.* Middletown, Conn.: Wesleyan Univ., 1928.

CL   *Contemporary Literature.* Madison: Univ. of Wisconsin, 1960.

CPEx   *Contemporary Poetry Explicator.* Teaneck, N.J.: Fairleigh Dickinson Univ., 1972.

EAL   *Early American Literature.* Amherst: Univ. of Massachusetts, 1966.

ESQ   *ESQ: A Journal of the American Renaissance.* Pullman: Washington State Univ., 1955.

Expl   *The Explicator.* Richmond: Virginia Commonwealth Univ., 1942.

GaR   *Georgia Review.* Athens: Univ. of Georgia, 1947.

HudR	*Hudson Review*. New York: Hudson Review, Inc., 1948.
KR	*Kenyon Review*. Gambier, Ohio: Kenyon College, 1939.
MissQ	*Mississippi Quarterly: A Journal of Southern Culture.* State College: Mississippi State Univ., 1947.
MFS	*Modern Fiction Studies*. Lafayette, Ind.: Purdue Univ., 1955.
NALF	*Negro American Literature Forum*. Terre Haute: Indiana State Univ., 1967.
NEQ	*New England Quarterly*. Brunswick, Me.: Colonial Society of Massachusetts and New England Quarterly, 1928.
NCF	*Nineteenth-Century Fiction*. Los Angeles: Univ. of California, 1945.
PMLA	*Publication of the Modern Language Association of America.* New York: Modern Language Association of America, 1885–.
PR	*Partisan Review*. New Brunswick, N.J.: Rutgers Univ., 1939.
RALS	*Resources for American Literary Study*. Richmond: Virginia Commonwealth Univ., and College Park: Univ. of Maryland, 1971.
SAQ	*South Atlantic Quarterly*. Durham, N.C.: Duke Univ. Press, 1940.
SR	*Sewanee Review*. Sewanee, Tenn.: Univ. of the South, 1892.
SLJ	*Southern Literary Journal*. Chapel Hill: Univ. of North Carolina, 1968.
SoR	*Southern Review*. Baton Rouge: Louisiana State Univ. Press, 1935.
SWAL	*Southwestern American Literature*. Denton: North Texas State Univ., 1972.
SAF	*Studies in American Fiction*. Boston: Northeastern Univ., 1973.
SAH	*Studies in American Humor*. San Marcos: Southwest Texas State Univ., 1975.
SBL	*Studies in Black Literature*. Fredericksburg, Va.: Mary Washington College, 1970.

SSF	*Studies in Short Fiction.* Newberry, Ga.: Newberry College, 1963.
SLI	*Studies in the Literary Imagination.* Atlanta: Georgia State Univ., 1968.
TSL	*Tennessee Studies in Literature.* Knoxville: Univ. of Tennessee, 1956.
TSLL	*Texas Studies in Literature and Language.* Austin: Univ. of Texas, 1959.
TSE	*Tulane Studies in English.* New Orleans: Tulane Univ., 1949.
TCL	*Twentieth-Century Literature.* Hempstead, N.Y.: Hofstra Univ., 1955.
VQR	*Virginia Quarterly Review.* Charlottesville: Univ. of Virginia, 1925.
WAL	*Western American Literature.* Logan: Utah State Univ., 1966.
WHR	*Western Humanities Review.* Salt Lake City: Univ. of Utah, 1947.
YR	*Yale Review.* New Haven: Yale Univ., 1911.

CHAPTER EIGHT
Bibliographical Guides

❦ ❦ ❦ There are so many bibliographies of American literature that it has taken more than four hundred double-column pages simply to list them in Charles Nilon, *Bibliography of Bibliographies of American Literature* (New York and London: Bowker, 1970) [Z1225/A1N5]. Every student will then turn with gratitude to the bibliographical volume of the *Literary History of the United States*, 4th ed., rev. (New York: Macmillan, 1974) [PS88/L522/1974] vol. 2, which contains in well-ordered detail virtually everything he will want to know about who said what about what or whom in discussing literature in America, where what was said was published, and usually how valuable or trustworthy the information is. Jacob Blanck, *Bibliography of American Literature* (New Haven: Yale

Univ. Press, 1955–) [Z1225/B55], when completed, will contain descriptive bibliographies of the writings of some three hundred prominent American authors.

Especially useful are six volumes in the Goldentree Bibliographies in Language and Literature series (New York: Appleton-Century-Crofts, 1966–1970): Richard Beale Davis, *American Literature through Bryant, 1585–1830* (1969) [Z1225/D3]; Harry Hayden Clark, *American Literature: Poe through Garland* (1971) [Z1227/C58]; C. Hugh Holman, *The American Novel through Henry James* (1966) [Z1231/F4H64]; Blake Nevius, *The American Novel: Sinclair Lewis to the Present* (1970) [Z1231/F4N4]; E. Hudson Long, *American Drama from Its Beginnings to the Present* (1970) [Z1231/D7L64]; and Darwin T. Turner, *Afro-American Writers* (1970) [Z1361/N39T78]. See also Howard Mumford Jones and Richard M. Ludwig, *Guide to American Literature and Its Backgrounds Since 1890*, 3rd ed. (Cambridge: Harvard Univ. Press, 1964) [Z1225/J65] and Louis D. Rubin, Jr., *A Bibliographical Guide to the Study of Southern Literature* (Baton Rouge: Louisiana State Univ. Press, 1969) [Z1225/S6R8].

Critical bibliographical essays on Edgar Allan Poe, Ralph Waldo Emerson, Nathaniel Hawthorne, Henry David Thoreau, Herman Melville, Walt Whitman, Mark Twain, and Henry James appear in Floyd Stovall, ed., *Eight American Authors: A Review of Research and Criticism* (New York: Modern Language Association, 1956) [PS201/S8/1963] and in the volume as revised and extended, James Woodress, ed. (New York: Norton, 1971) [PS201/E4/1971]. This was followed by a companion volume, Robert A. Rees and Earl N. Harbert, eds., *Fifteen American Authors before 1900: Bibliographic Essays on Research and Criticism* (Madison: Univ. of Wisconsin Press, 1971) [PS201/R44] and by Jackson R. Bryer, ed., *Fifteen Modern American Authors: A Survey of Research and Criticism* (Durham, N.C.: Duke Univ. Press, 1969) [PS221/B7], revised and enlarged as *Sixteen Modern American Authors: A Survey of Research and Criticism* (New York: Norton, 1973) [PS221/B7/1974].

A listing of writings on American literature appears annually in the *International Bibliography of Books and Articles on the Modern Languages and Literatures* [Z7006/M64], published since 1921 by the Modern Language Association of America. Since 1963, each year's writing has been reviewed in bibliographical essays in James L. Woodress, later J. Albert Robbins, ed., *American Literary Scholarship: An Annual* (Durham, N.C.: Duke Univ. Press, 1963–) [PS3/ A47]. The quarterly *American Literature Abstracts* (1967–) is devoted to "a review of current scholarship." A section on American literature is also included in *Abstracts of English Studies* (1958–). *American Literary Realism* (1967–) presents annotated bibliographies of secondary material on writers who flourished between 1867 and 1910. Also see the essays and checklists in each issue of *Resources for American Literary Study* (1971–).

Each issue of *American Literature* (1929–) lists "Articles on American Literature Appearing in Current Periodicals." Other annual or quarterly listings will be found in *Mississippi Quarterly* (1947–), *Modern Drama* (1958–), *Modern Fiction Studies* (1955–), and *Western American Literature* (1965–). More comprehensive listings are Lewis Leary, *Articles on American Literature, 1900–1950* (Durham, N.C.: Duke Univ. Press, 1954) [Z1225/L48] and his *Articles on American Literature, 1950–1967* (Durham, N.C.: Duke Univ. Press, 1970) [Z1225/L492]. A third volume covering the years 1968 through 1975 is now in progress.

The standard guide to materials in general American magazines is *Reader's Guide to Periodical Literature* (1900–). It appears semimonthly and is then cumulated into annual and biennial volumes. For earlier years, from 1802–1907, consult *Poole's Index to Periodical Literature*. Selected book reviews from American periodicals are indexed, digested, and often quoted in *Book Review Digest* (1905–). The most useful and usually most available newspaper index is the *New York Times Index* (1931–).

James Woodress, *Dissertations in American Literature* (Durham, N.C.: Duke Univ. Press, 1962) [Z1225/W8/1962] is a classified list of all doctoral dissertations completed through 1961 at more than one hundred universities in the United States and abroad. An incomplete but useful listing of current doctoral dissertations, completed or proposed, appears quarterly in the abovementioned *American Literature*. Joseph Jones, *American Literary Manuscripts: A Checklist of Holdings in the United States* (Austin: Univ. of Texas Press, 1960) [Z6620/U5M6] is being revised and enlarged by a committee of the American literature section of the Modern Language Association of America under the direction of J. Albert Robbins.

CHAPTER NINE
Biographical Sources

ᘐ ᘐ ᘐ So many collections of biographical sketches of notable Americans have appeared that the student who wishes to find them all must go to Marion Dargan, *Guide to American Biography*, 2 vols. (Albuquerque: Univ. of New Mexico Press, 1949, 1952) [Z5305/ U5D32]. For biographical material in recently published books or magazines, the student should consult the quarterly *Biography Index* (1946–). For biographical information provided by living Americans, go to *Who's Who in America* (Chicago: Marquis, issued biennially since 1899) [E663/W56]. For information on people who have been in *Who's Who in America* but have died, there is the companion *Who Was Who in America* [E176/W64], containing the same biographical information but "with dates of death appended."

Evert A. and George L. Duyckinck, *Cyclopaedia of American Literature; Embracing Personal and Critical Notices of Authors, and Selections from Their Writings. From the Earliest Period to the Present Day; with Portraits, Autographs, and Other Illustrations* (New York: Scribner, 1855) [PS85/D6], several times reprinted, is especially valuable because many writers of the mid-nineteenth century were apparently given opportunities to revise, or even compose, statements about themselves. *Appleton's Cyclopaedia of American Biography*, edited by James Grant Wilson and John Fisk in seven volumes (New York: Appleton, 1887–1901), issued in an enlarged edition in 1915, and with supplementary volumes appearing in 1931 [E176/A65], contains biographical information on some writers not listed in the standard *Dictionary of American Biography*, compiled under the auspices of the American Council of Learned Societies, first by Allen Johnson (1926–1931), then by Dumas Malone (1929–1937), and published in twenty volumes and an index volume (New York: Scribner's, 1928–1937) [E176/D56]. Living people are not included in the *DAB*. Three supplementary volumes have appeared—the first in 1944, Harris E. Starr, ed., containing sketches of Americans who had died before 1935; the second in 1958, Robert L. Schuyler, ed., concerning those who died before 1940; and a third in 1973, Edward T. James, ed., bringing the work through 1945.

The standard one-volume reference since it first appeared in 1941 is James D. Hart, *The Oxford Companion to American Literature,* 5th ed. (New York: Oxford Univ. Press, 1975) [PS21/H3/1975]. Less consistently reliable, but also useful, are Max Herzberg and others, *The Reader's Encyclopedia of American Literature* (New York: Crowell, 1962) [PS21/R4] and Stanley J. Kunitz and Howard Haycraft, *American Authors, 1600–1900: A Biographical Dictionary of American Literature* (New York: Wilson, 1938) [PS21/K8]. The latter also includes information on the "writing, selling, and preservation of American books."

The University of Minnesota Pamphlets on American Writers series (Minneapolis: Univ. of Minnesota Press) [PN4877/W45] has since 1959 presented brief biographical and critical introductions to more than ninety authors, most of which have been gathered by

Leonard Unger in *American Writers: A Collection of Literary Biographies* (New York: Scribner's, 1974) [PS129/A55]. Twayne's United States Authors Series (New York: Twayne, 1961–) has issued longer biographical and critical studies on more than two hundred writers.

CHAPTER TEN
Major American Writers

❦ ❦ ❦ Who are the major American writers? That question has bothered critics for almost two centuries, and no two generations have agreed on the answer. Hundreds of names have, at one time or another, been nominated. Only a few appear consistently in even a majority of polls taken among general readers or literary scholars.

The question has been asked again by the veteran scholar Jay B. Hubbell in *Who Are the Major American Writers? A Study of the Changing Literary Canon* (Durham, N.C.: Duke Univ. Press, 1972) [PS62/H8], a survey of widely diverging opinions from the early nineteenth century through the 1960s. The bibliographical volume of the *Literary History of the United States* surveys the writings of and criticisms on more than two hundred prominent authors. The as yet incomplete *Bibliography of American Literature* [Z1225/B55] will contain listings on the writings of some three hundred American writers who died before 1931. Some index of changes in public estimation may be suggested by recalling those writers who have been admitted to the Hall of Fame of Great Americans, which is maintained under the trusteeship of New York University. On its founding in 1900, Jonathan Edwards, Ralph Waldo Emerson, Benjamin Franklin, Nathaniel Hawthorne, Washington Irving, and Henry Wadsworth Longfellow were admitted; five years later James Russell Lowell and John Greenleaf Whittier were added, and in 1910 William Cullen Bryant, James Fenimore Cooper, Oliver Wendell Holmes, Edgar Allan Poe, and Harriet Beecher Stowe were admitted. Mark Twain was admitted in 1920, only ten years after his death, but Walt Whitman had to wait until 1930, almost forty years after his death, followed in 1945 by Sidney Lanier and Thomas Paine. Henry David Thoreau was not admitted until 1965.

No abbreviated list of the most important American writers will satisfy everyone, but there has been in our time a kind of consensus in which forty-five of them have been recently named and examined in detailed bibliographical essays. Everett H. Emerson, ed., *Major Writers of Early American Literature* (Madison: Univ. of Wisconsin Press, 1972) [PS185/E4] provides a fresh appraisal of nine important writers of seventeenth- and eighteenth-century America: William Bradford, Ann Bradstreet, Edward Taylor, Cotton Mather, William Byrd, Jonathan Edwards, Benjamin Franklin, Philip Freneau, and Charles Brockden Brown. But even in so generous an offering, some students have wondered why Captain John Smith was not included, or Hector St. John Crèvecoeur, William Bartram, Royall Tyler, Joseph Dennie, or such prominent early New Englanders as John Trumbull, Timothy Dwight, and Joel Barlow. For the latter three, however, see Leon Howard, *The Connecticut Wits* (Chicago: Univ. of Chicago Press, 1943) [PS193/H6], one of the more illuminating of modern literary studies. Lewis Leary, *Soundings: Some Early American Writers* (Athens: Univ. of Georgia Press, 1975) [PS193/L4] speaks of other late eighteenth-century and early nineteenth-century writers.

James Woodress, ed., *Eight American Authors: A Review of Re-*

search and Criticism, rev. ed. (New York: Norton, 1971) [PS201/
E4/1971] contains authoritative bibliographical essays on Edgar
Allan Poe, Ralph Waldo Emerson, Nathaniel Hawthorne, Henry
David Thoreau, Herman Melville, Walt Whitman, Mark Twain,
and Henry James, writers considered to be the most important by
an informal consensus among scholars.

Robert A. Rees and Earl N. Harbert, eds., *Fifteen American
Authors before 1900: Bibliographic Essays on Research and Criti-
cism* (Madison: Univ. of Wisconsin Press, 1971) [PS201/R44]
extends that listing to include Henry Adams, William Cullen
Bryant, James Fenimore Cooper, Stephen Crane, Emily Dickinson,
Henry Wadsworth Longfellow, James Russell Lowell, Frank Norris,
and John Greenleaf Whittier, as well as Jonathan Edwards, Benjamin
Franklin, and Edward Taylor, three authors who have already been
mentioned as receiving similar bibliographic treatment in *Major
Writers of Early American Literature*.

Jackson Bryer, ed., *Sixteen Modern American Authors: A Survey
of Research and Criticism* (New York: Norton, 1974) [PS221/B7/
1974] selects as important twentieth-century American writers
Sherwood Anderson, Willa Cather, Hart Crane, Theodore Dreiser,
T. S. Eliot, William Faulkner, Robert Frost, Ernest Hemingway,
Eugene O'Neill, Ezra Pound, Edwin Arlington Robinson, John
Steinbeck, Wallace Stevens, William Carlos Williams, and Thomas
Wolfe. Once again, however, there are complaints that significant
writers have been left out of this list. Where, for example, is Edith
Wharton, Carl Sandburg, Gertrude Stein, Thornton Wilder, or
John Dos Passos? Why is Eugene O'Neill the only playwright listed
in any of the four volumes mentioned?

To decide which writers should be spoken of in some detail in
the present resource guide, thirty prominent scholar-teachers from
all sections of the United States were each asked to name the twenty
writers that they considered the most important for the undergraduate
student of American literature to know. Fifteen younger instructors
actively engaged in teaching American literature to undergraduates
were asked the same question, and fifty undergraduate students
majoring in English were also asked. Their replies resulted in a
list of more than two hundred writers, ranging from Anne Bradstreet
to Joyce Carol Oates, from Jonathan Edwards to Ken Kesey. Even
the thirty scholar-teachers could not agree. The only writers receiv-

ing unanimous recommendation in their listings were Nathaniel Hawthorne and Herman Melville. So close was the voting that a final tabulation made necessary the selection of, not twenty, but twenty-three writers who by consensus were, or should be, most important for undergraduate students of American literature to know.

What has been said about these twenty-three writers is reviewed below, with the writers' names appearing in alphabetical order. In addition, there is a twenty-fourth section on the familiar "Schoolroom Poets" of the nineteenth century (John Greenleaf Whittier, Henry Wadsworth Longfellow, James Russell Lowell, and Oliver Wendell Holmes), who were so conspicuously a part of an emerging national literature that, though less universally esteemed today, they should not be forgotten. For other writers whom many people will inevitably feel should have been included, excellent guidance can be found in the six volumes of the Goldentree Bibliographies and in the other references mentioned under "Bibliographical Guides," pp. 64–66, above. In addition to these, any of the standard encyclopedias will supply sound information and leads to further sources of information.

SAMUEL LANGHORNE CLEMENS (1835–1910)

Everyone seems to be writing about Mark Twain. His own writings, published and unpublished, are being issued in impeccably edited volumes by the University of California Press in two series, The Works of Mark Twain, projected in twenty-four volumes, and The Mark Twain Papers, which will fill at least fifteen volumes more. Books and articles about him appear with increasing regularity, their quality as unpredictable as Twain himself. People quarrel about him, as Van Wyck Brooks, *The Ordeal of Mark Twain*, rev. ed. (New York: Dutton, 1923) [PS1331/B7/1933] and Bernard DeVoto, *Mark Twain's America* (Boston: Little, Brown, 1932) [PS1331/D4] quarreled over whether Clemens was an artist thwarted by his time and place or a genuine native genius; critical reverberations from this quarrel, as other critics took sides, are collected in Lewis Leary, ed., *A Casebook on Mark Twain's Wound* (New York: Crowell, 1962) [PS1331/L42]. Others quarreled over whether Mark Twain lost much of his magic as he grew older: Hamlin Hill, *Mark*

Twain: God's Fool (New York: Harper & Row, 1973) [PS1332/ H5] suspects that he did; Maxwell Geismar, *Mark Twain: An American Prophet* (Boston: Houghton Mifflin, 1970) [PS1331/ G4], dogmatically asserts that he did not. Robert A. Wiggins, *Mark Twain: Jackleg Novelist* (Seattle: Univ. of Washington Press, 1964) [PS1331/W5] finds him a clumsy wielder of the tools of his trade; others point to his superb craftsmanship. "All modern American literature," said Ernest Hemingway in the first chapter of *The Green Hills of Africa* (New York: Scribner's, 1935) [PS3515/E37G74/ 1935], "comes from one book by Mark Twain called *Huckleberry Finn.*"

The most complete modern account of his life is Justin Kaplan, *Mr. Clemens and Mark Twain: A Biography* (New York: Simon and Schuster, 1966) [PS1331/K33], a readable account that is not altogether popular among some scholars, who find bias in it and distortion of fact. Many of them return, but with caution, to what Clemens's literary executor, Albert Bigelow Paine, said in often undiscriminating praise of the author in *Mark Twain, a Biography: The Personal and Literary Life of Samuel Langhorne Clemens*, 3 vols. (New York: Harper, 1912) [PS1331/P3/1912]. Perhaps the most safely satisfactory biography, however, is De Lancey Ferguson, *Mark Twain: Man and Legend* (Indianapolis: Bobbs-Merrill, 1943) [PS1331/F4]. Edward Wagenknecht, *Mark Twain: The Man and the Work*, rev. ed. (Norman: Univ. of Oklahoma Press, 1961) [PS1331/W3] is a comfortable book, mediatory rather than judicial, and quietly useful. Frank Baldanza, *Mark Twain: An Introduction and Interpretation* (New York: Barnes and Noble, 1961) [PS1331/B3] and Lewis Leary, *Mark Twain* (Minneapolis: Univ. of Minnesota Press, 1960) [PS1331/L43] are also useful and brief.

Various periods of Mark Twain's life are covered in generous detail in, among others, Dixon Wecter, *Sam Clemens of Hannibal* (Boston: Houghton Mifflin, 1952) [PS1332/W40]; Edgar M. Branch, *The Literary Apprenticeship of Mark Twain, with Selections from his Apprentice Writing* (Urbana: Univ. of Illinois Press, 1950) [PS1332/B7]; Ivan Benson, *Mark Twain's Western Years* (Stanford: Stanford Univ. Press, 1938) [PS1332/B4]; Dewey Ganzel, *Mark Twain Abroad: The Cruise of the Quaker City* (Chicago: Univ. of Chicago Press, 1968) [PS1332/G3]; Paul Fatout, *Mark*

Twain on the Lecture Circuit (Bloomington: Indiana Univ. Press, 1960) [PS1331/F3]; Kenneth R. Andrews, *Nook Farm: Mark Twain's Hartford Circle* (Cambridge: Harvard Univ. Press, 1950) [PS1334/A6]; Samuel ·Charles Webster, *Mark Twain, Business Man* (Boston: Little, Brown, 1946) [PS1331/A3W4]; and, for the later years, Hamlin Hill, *Mark Twain: God's Fool*, already mentioned.

Other books speak of his relationships with friends or associates: Margaret Duckett, *Mark Twain and Bret Harte* (Norman: Univ. of Oklahoma Press, 1964) [PS1333/D8]; Arlin Turner, *Mark Twain and George W. Cable: The Records of a Literary Friendship* (East Lansing: Michigan State Univ. Press, 1960) [PS1246/A55]; Hamlin Hill, *Mark Twain and Elisha Bliss* (Columbia: Univ. of Missouri Press, 1964) [PS1334/H5]; and, most valuable, Henry Nash Smith and William M. Gibson, eds., *Mark Twain-Howells Letters: The Correspondence of Samuel L. Clemens and William Dean Howells, 1872–1910*, 2 vols. (Cambridge: Belknap Press of Harvard Univ. Press, 1960) [PS1331/A3H6].

Critical studies are numerous. Henry Nash Smith, *Mark Twain: The Development of a Writer* (Cambridge: Belknap Press of Harvard Univ. Press, 1962) [PS1331/S55/1962] is considered by many to be the most soundly inclusive. Others prefer James M. Cox, *Mark Twain: The Fate of Humor* (Princeton: Princeton Univ. Press, 1966) [PS1331/C6], which is especially good in its discussion of *Adventures of Huckleberry Finn*. Inevitably, much of the best criticism has focused on this, Mark Twain's best book, which has also been the cause of some of the most contentious quarrels, especially about whether its ending was appropriate to the rest of the book. Lionel Trilling, in an introduction to an edition of *Adventures of Huckleberry Finn* (New York: Rinehart, 1948) [PZ3/C59A52] and T. S. Eliot, in an introduction to another edition (New York: Chanticleer, 1950) [PZ3/C59A1], said it was; they were soundly taken to task by Leo Marx, "Mr. Eliot, Mr. Trilling, and Huckleberry Finn," *American Scholar*, 22 (August 1953), 423–40, and many others joined the fray. Lauriat Lane, "Why *Huckleberry Finn* is a Great World Novel," *College English*, 17 (October 1955), 1–5, was countered by William Van O'Connor, "Why *Huckleberry Finn* Is Not the Great American Novel," *College English*, 17 (October 1955), 6–10.

Walter Blair, *Mark Twain & Huck Finn* (Berkeley: Univ. of California Press, 1960) [PS1305/B5] is a monument of critical scholarship that examines the origins of the book in Samuel Clemens's boyhood experiences and the "ways he manipulated and augmented them when he transmuted them to fiction," and reveals where and when portions of the book were written. Other outstanding criticism includes Leslie Fiedler, "Come Back to the Raft Ag'in Huck Honey!" *Partisan Review*, 15 (June 1948), 664–71; James M. Cox, "Remarks on the Sad Initiation of Huckleberry Finn," *Sewanee Review*, 62 (Summer 1954), 389–405; Chadwick Hansen, "The Character of Jim and the Ending of Huckleberry Finn," *Massachusetts Review*, 5 (August 1963), 45–66; and Robert Penn Warren, "Mark Twain," *Southern Review*, 8 (July 1972), 459–92. E. Hudson Long, *Mark Twain Handbook* (New York: Hendricks, 1957) [PS1331/L6] is an indispensable guide to further studies.

There are three excellent critical editions: Sculley Bradley and others, eds., *The Adventures of Huckleberry Finn: An Annotated Text, Backgrounds and Sources, Essays in Criticism* (New York: Norton, 1962) [PZ3/C59A68]; Richard Lettis, Robert F. McDonnell, and William E. Morris, eds., *Huck Finn and His Critics* (New York: Macmillan, 1962) [PZ3/C59/A70]; and, perhaps best, Hamlin Hill and Walter Blair, *The Art of Huckleberry Finn, Texts, Sources, Criticism* (San Francisco: Chandler, 1969) [PS1305/A1/1969], which contains a facsimile of the illustrated first edition of the novel.

An important oblique commentary is John Seelye, *The True Adventures of Huckleberry Finn* (Evanston, Ill.: Northwestern Univ. Press, 1970) [PS3569/E35T7], a retelling of "the story like it really happened, leaving in all the cuss words and the sex and the sadness," with a spare page at the end so that every critical reader can supply a conclusion of his own. Huck explains that "Mark Twain's book is for children and such, whilst this here one is for crickits."

Useful collections of critical essays include Justin Kaplan, ed., *Mark Twain: A Profile* (New York: Hill and Wang, 1967) [PS1331/K32]; Guy A. Cardwell, ed., *Discussions of Mark Twain* (Boston: Heath, 1963) [PS1331/C3]; and Arthur L. Scott, ed., *Mark Twain: Selected Criticism* (Dallas: Southern Methodist Univ. Press, 1955) [PS1331/S3].

JAMES FENIMORE COOPER (1789–1851)

Literary scholars are just beginning to catch up with Cooper, viewing him in a more appreciative light now than they often had in the past. *The Works of James Fenimore Cooper* has been projected by the State Univ. of New York Press. James Franklin Beard, ed., *The Letters and Journals of James Fenimore Cooper*, 6 vols. (Cambridge: Belknap Press of Harvard Univ. Press, 1960–1968) [PS1431/A3/1960] has revealed important new information about the novelist's life and writings. But, so far, no completely satisfactory biography has appeared. The best presently available is James Grossman, *James Fenimore Cooper* (New York: Sloane, 1949) [PS1431/G77/1949]. Shorter sources of biographical information are Donald A. Ringe, *James Fenimore Cooper* (New York: Twayne, 1962) [PS1438/R5]; Warren S. Walker, *James Fenimore Cooper: An Introduction and Interpretation* (New York: Barnes and Noble, 1962) [PS1431/W3]; and Robert E. Spiller, *James Fenimore Cooper* (Minneapolis: Univ. of Minnesota Press, 1965) [PS1431/S63].

A seminal study, Robert E. Spiller, *Fenimore Cooper: Critic of His Times* (New York: Minton, Balch, 1931) [PS1431/S6], is less a "biography in the ordinary sense" than the "record of the evolution of a point of view"; see also Spiller's mildly corrective "Second Thoughts on Cooper as a Social Critic," *New York History*, 35 (October 1954), 540–47. Dorothy Waples, *The Whig Myth of Fenimore Cooper* (New Haven: Yale Univ. Press, 1938) [PS1433/W3/1938] surveys the public image of the novelist during his later years. Kay Seymour House, *Cooper's Americans* (Columbus: Ohio State Univ. Press, 1965) [PS1439/H6] is a thoughtful revelation of the social backgrounds of Cooper's fiction and may well be the single most useful introduction to his writings.

Arvid Shulenberger, *Cooper's Theory of Fiction: His Prefaces and Their Relation to His Novels* (Lawrence: Univ. of Kansas Press, 1955) [PS1438/S5] continues to be useful, but it should be supplemented by such influential critiques as those found in Marius Bewley, "Revaluations: James Fenimore Cooper," *Scrutiny*, 19 (Winter 1952–1953), 98–125, reprinted in *The Eccentric Design: Form in the Classic American Novel* (New York: Columbia Univ. Press, 1959) [PS371/B4]; Howard Mumford Jones, "James

Fenimore Cooper: A Re-Appraisal," *New York History*, 35 (October 1954), 369–73; and by discussions of Cooper in Richard Chase, *The American Novel and Its Traditions* (Garden City: Doubleday, 1957) [PS371/C5]; and especially Leslie Fiedler, *Love and Death in the American Novel* (New York: Criterion, 1960) [PS374/L6F5]; Edwin Fussell, *Frontier: American Literature and the American West* (Princeton: Princeton Univ. Press, 1965) [PS169/W4F5]; D. H. Lawrence, *Studies in Classic American Literature* (New York: Thomas Seltzer, 1923) [PS121/L3]; and Tony Tanner, *The Reign of Wonder: Naivety and Reality in American Fiction* (Cambridge: Cambridge Univ. Press, 1965) [PS88/T25].

George Dekker, *James Fenimore Cooper: The Novelist* (London: Routledge & Paul, 1967), in the American edition titled *James Fenimore Cooper: The American Scott* (New York: Barnes and Noble, 1967) [PS1438/D4/1967b], argues that Cooper was indeed "the American Walter Scott," that he was not "a novelist of the very first rank," but that his fiction reveals "real strengths . . . great and richly compensating." The influence of painting on Cooper's fiction and his fine knowledge and appreciation of art is touched on in Howard Mumford Jones, "James Fenimore Cooper and the Hudson River School," *Magazine of Art*, 44 (October 1954), 243–51. His later achievement as a pioneer writer on the sea is set forth in Thomas Philbrick, *James Fenimore Cooper and the Development of American Sea Fiction* (Cambridge: Harvard Univ. Press, 1961) [PS1442/S4P45]. Frank M. Collins, "Cooper and the American Dream," *Publication of the Modern Language Association*, 81 (March 1966), 79–94 reveals native backgrounds of his thought.

Do not miss Mark Twain's hilarious "Fenimore Cooper's Literary Offenses," *North American Review*, 161 (July 1895), 1–12, and often reprinted, or its sequel, "Fenimore Cooper's Further Literary Offenses," *New England Quarterly*, 19 (September 1946), 291–301, both discussed in Sydney J. Krause, "Cooper's Literary Offenses: Mark Twain in Wonderland," *New England Quarterly*, 38 (September 1965), 291–311.

STEPHEN CRANE (1871–1900)

The Works of Stephen Crane [PS1449/C85/1969] has been published in 10 volumes by the University Press of Virginia. Joseph

Katz, ed., *The Poems of Stephen Crane: A Critical Edition* (New York: Cooper Square, 1966) [PS1449/C85A17/1966] is an authoritative, though incomplete, collection with a distinguished introduction. R. W. Stallman and E. R. Hagemann, eds., *The War Dispatches of Stephen Crane* (New York: New York Univ. Press, 1964) [PS1449/C85Z5] brings together Crane's writings as a foreign correspondent during the Greco-Turkish, the Spanish-American, and the Boer wars. R. W. Stallman and Lillian Gilkes, eds., *Stephen Crane: Letters* (New York: New York Univ. Press, 1960) [PS1449/C85Z54], though incomplete, reveals some of the interesting paradoxes in Crane's volatile personality, conscientious but at the same time irresponsible, egocentric and eager for success, yet openhanded in generosity among his friends. Stanley Wertheim, "Stephen Crane," in Theodore L. Gross and Stanley Wertheim, *Hawthorne, Melville, Stephen Crane: A Critical Bibliography* (New York: Free Press, 1971) [Z1225/G76], presents a detailed, judicious, and indispensable summary of the important books and articles that have been written about Crane. More comprehensive but somewhat biased is R. W. Stallman, *Stephen Crane: A Critical Bibliography* (Ames: Iowa State Univ. Press, 1972) [Z8198/2/S76].

The most complete biography is Robert W. Stallman, *Stephen Crane: A Biography** (New York: Braziller, 1968) [PS1449/C85Z9], a study based on years of intensive work following every phase of Crane's career, which not only details his life story but also contains analyses and evaluations of Crane's more important narratives. John Berryman, *Stephen Crane* (New York: Sloane, 1950; rpt. with a new preface, Cleveland: Meridian, 1962) [PS1449/C85Z56], is a poet's sensitive but sometimes eccentric Freudian interpretation of the relationship between Crane's private life and his public writings. Corwin K. Linson, *My Stephen Crane*, ed. Edwin H. Cady (Syracuse: Syracuse Univ. Press, 1958) [PS1449/C85Z73] is an informal, reminiscent account of Crane's earliest productive years written by an artist who knew him when he was struggling for public recognition. Lillian Gilkes, *Cora Crane: A Biography of Mrs. Stephen Crane* (Bloomington: Indiana Univ. Press, 1960) [PS1449/C85Z63] is a woman's-eye view of the woman who did much to sustain Crane during the years of his decline. More objective is Eric Solomon, *Stephen Crane in England: A Portrait of the Artist* (Columbus: Ohio State Univ. Press, 1964)

[PS1449/C85Z85], which explains the influences on Crane of such transatlantic associates as Henry James and Joseph Conrad. Edwin H. Cady, *Stephen Crane** (New York: Twayne, 1962) [PS1449/C85Z575], though not profound and sometimes eccentric—as when he stresses the aristocratic and Christian qualities of Crane's artistic vision—presents an adequate brief introduction to the man and the writings and contains a useful bibliography.

Many students find Daniel G. Hoffman, *The Poetry of Stephen Crane** (New York: Columbia Univ. Press, 1957) [PS1449/C85Z65], though focused on Crane's verse, to be the most satisfactory critical introduction to the whole of his writings, pointing to themes (man versus God, love, war, and social injustice) that underlie Crane's most effective writing. The first, and still the most important, full-length study of Crane's short stories and novels is Eric Solomon, *Stephen Crane: From Parody to Realism* (Cambridge: Harvard Univ. Press, 1966) [PS1449/C85Z848], which presents effective analyses of individual works and emphasizes the notion that Crane's most effective instrument is ironic social commentary. Donald B. Gibson, *The Fiction of Stephen Crane* (Carbondale: Southern Illinois Univ. Press, 1968) [PS1449/C85Z62] is an interesting exercise in depth psychology, which speculates more about the neuroses of the man than about the quality of his writings. Crane's fiction can perhaps best be approached through Charles C. Walcutt, "Stephen Crane: Naturalist and Impressionist," in *American Literary Naturalism: A Divided Stream* (Minneapolis: Univ. of Minnesota Press, 1956) [PS379/W28], pp. 66–80; James B. Colvert, "Structure and Theme in Crane's Fiction," *Modern Fiction Studies,* 5 (August 1959), 199–208; or Thomas A. Gullason, "Thematic Patterns in Stephen Crane's Early Novels," *Nineteenth-Century Fiction,* 16 (June 1961), 59–67. Each of these efforts contains insightful, judicious appraisals.

The introduction to Robert W. Stallman, ed., *The Red Badge of Courage** (New York: Modern Library, 1951) [PZ3/C852R12], which identifies Crane's best-known novel as an allegory, mythic and ritualistic, held together by a framework of Christian symbolism with the soldier Jim Conklin as a redeeming Christ figure, set in motion a stream of controversy that still, though diminishing, dominates much Crane criticism. See, for example, Eric Solomon, "The Structure of 'The Red Badge of Courage,'" *Modern Fiction*

Studies, 5 (August 1959), 220–234, which takes a position much like Stallman's; but see also Philip Rahv, "Fiction and the Criticism of Fiction," *Kenyon Review*, 18 (Spring 1956), 276–99, which urges that what symbolism there is in the novel is merely an adjunct to the novel's primary concern with a representation of reality. The controversy over whether *The Red Badge of Courage* is symbolistic, allegorical, naturalistic, or realistic still goes on, testimony, perhaps, to the fact that Crane is, at least in that work, a novelist of intriguing complexity.

EMILY DICKINSON (1830–1886)

Patient, scholarly housecleaning has cleared up much of the disarray that, until recently, characterized testimony on Dickinson's life and writings. Thomas H. Johnson, ed., *The Poems of Emily Dickinson, Including Variant Readings Critically Compared with All Known Manuscripts*, 3 vols. (Cambridge: Belknap Press of Harvard Univ. Press, 1955) [PS1541/A1/1955] definitively establishes the text of her 1775 poems, some in variant versions; an addendum to this canon is David M. Higgins, ed., "Twenty-five Poems by Emily Dickinson: Unpublished Variant Version," *American Literature*, 38 (March 1966), 1–21. Thomas H. Johnson, *The Complete Poems of Emily Dickinson* (Boston: Little, Brown, 1960) [PS1541/A1/1960] presents a single version of all known poems, and his *Final Harvest: Emily Dickinson's Poems* (Boston: Little, Brown, 1961) [PS1541/A133] is a selection of 575 poems that best represent the poet. Thomas H. Johnson and Theodora Ward, eds., *The Letters of Emily Dickinson*, 3 vols. (Cambridge: Belknap Press of Harvard Univ. Press, 1958) [PS1541/Z5A3] supersedes previous collections of her letters; Thomas H. Johnson, ed., *Emily Dickinson: Selected Letters* (Cambridge: Belknap Press of Harvard Univ. Press, 1971) [PS1541/Z5A32] derives from the previous, more complete, edition. Jay Leyda, *The Years and Hours of Emily Dickinson*, 2 vols. (New Haven: Yale Univ. Press, 1960) [PS1541/Z5L4], presenting a day-by-day account of the poet's quiet activities, documents important biographical facts. Based on all these and more, Richard B. Sewall, *The Life of Emily Dickinson*, 2 vols. (New York: Farrar, Straus, and Giroux, 1974) [PS1541/Z55S42] is the complete biography that had long been awaited. Almost all previous biographical accounts had been marred by speculation or bias.

There were important exceptions. Thomas H. Johnson, *Emily Dickinson: An Interpretive Biography** (Cambridge: Belknap Press of Harvard Univ. Press, 1955) [PS1541/Z5J6] examines the poetry for its revelation of the artist's inner life. Theodora Ward, *The Capsule of the Mind: Chapters in the Life of Emily Dickinson* (Cambridge: Belknap Press of Harvard Univ. Press, 1961) [PS1541/Z5W3] contains six attractive essays on the poet's life and friendships. Still valuable as a sensitive introduction, and reliable except in speculation about the men in Dickinson's life, is George Whicher, *This Was a Poet: A Critical Biography of Emily Dickinson* (New York: Scribner's, 1938) [PS1541/Z5W5]; also see Genevieve Taggard, *The Life and Mind of Emily Dickinson* (New York: Knopf, 1930) [PS1541/Z5T3], which presents a poet's sympathetic view of another poet. Somewhat marred by too much attention to identifying people to whom Dickinson directed her love poems are David Higgins, *Portrait of Emily Dickinson: The Poet and Her Prose* (New Brunswick, N.J.: Rutgers Univ. Press, 1967) [PS1541/Z5H5] and Ruth Miller, *The Poetry of Emily Dickinson* (Middleton, Conn.: Wesleyan Univ. Press, 1968) [PS1541/Z5M5]. Both, however, contain enlivening criticism stretched on a biographical framework. Henry W. Wells, *Introduction to Emily Dickinson** (Chicago: Hendricks, 1947) [PS1541/Z5W4], though sometimes overwhelmingly appreciative, is a useful introductory volume, as are John R. Pickard, *Emily Dickinson: An Introduction and Interpretation* (New York: Barnes and Noble, 1947) [PS1541/Z5P5] and Denis Donoghue, *Emily Dickinson** (Minneapolis: Univ. of Minnesota Press, 1969) [PS1541/Z5D6].

There are numerous discerning critical studies. Richard Chase, *Emily Dickinson* (New York: Sloane, 1951) [PS1541/Z5C5] contains discriminating, if austere, interpretive judgments. Charles R. Anderson, *Emily Dickinson's Poetry: Stairway of Surprise* (New York: Holt, Rinehart & Winston, 1960) [PS1541/Z5A63] offers thoughtful readings of 103 of Dickinson's "really fine poems." Clark Griffith, *The Long Shadow: Emily Dickinson's Tragic Poetry* (Princeton: Princeton Univ. Press, 1963) [PS1541/Z5G7] studies more than fifty poems that reveal Dickinson as a person who shared with Herman Melville a sense of the human predicament in a world that "thwarts his cravings and remains deaf to his appeals." David T. Porter, *The Art of Emily Dickinson's Early Poems* (Cambridge: Harvard Univ. Press, 1966) [PS1541/Z5P] closely examines 301 poems written before 1862. William R. Sherwood, *Circumference and Circumstance: Stages in the Mind and Art of Emily Dickinson* (New York: Columbia Univ. Press, 1968) [PS1541/Z5S5] uses textual analysis "to suggest how central and radical a figure she is in the sweep of the American imagination." Brita Lindberg-Seyersted, *The Voice of the Poet: Aspects of Style in the Poetry of Emily Dickinson* (Cambridge: Harvard Univ. Press, 1968) [PS1541/Z5L5/1968] reveals "stylistic elements at several levels of the poet's language" by appropriating "theories and methods of modern linguistics in analysis."

Perhaps the most completely useful critical volume is Albert J. Gelpi, *Emily Dickinson: The Mind of the Poet** (Cambridge: Harvard Univ. Press, 1965) [PS1541/Z5G4], especially in its chapter on "Seeing New Englandly: From Edwards to Emerson to Dickinson," which places Dickinson securely within a native literary tradition. Modern poets speak well of her in Archibald MacLeish, Louise Bogan, and Richard Wilbur, *Emily Dickinson: Three Views* (Amherst, Mass.: Amherst College Press, 1960) [PS1541/Z5A6]. Incisive critical essays include R. P. Blackmur, "Emily Dickinson," *Southern Review*, 2 (Autumn 1937), 325–47; F. O. Matthiessen, "The Problem of a Private Poet," *Kenyon Review*, 7 (Autumn 1945), 584–97; Allen Tate, "New England Culture and Emily Dickinson," *Symposium*, 3 (April 1932), 206–26; Austin Warren, "Emily Dickinson," *Sewanee Review*, 45 (August 1957), 568–86; and, as a corrective to deluges of praise, Yvor Winters, "Emily Dickinson and the Limits of Judgment," in *Maule's Curse: Seven Studies in the History of American Obscurantism* (Norfolk, Conn.: New Directions, 1938) [PS201/W5].

Critical essays are collected in Caesar R. Blake and Carlton F. Wells, eds., *The Recognition of Emily Dickinson: Selected Criticism since 1890** (Ann Arbor: Univ. of Michigan Press, 1964) [PS1541/Z5B55] and Richard B. Sewall, ed., *Emily Dickinson: A Collection of Critical Essays* (Englewood Cliffs, N.J.: Prentice-Hall, 1966) [PS1541/Z5S4]. Listings of almost everything written by or about the poet are Sheila T. Clendinning, ed., *Emily Dickinson: A Bibliography: 1850–1966* (Kent, Ohio: Kent State Univ. Press, 1968)

[Z8230/5/C55] and Willis J. Buckingham, ed., *Emily Dickinson: An Annotated Bibliography. Writings, Scholarship, Criticism and Ana, 1850–1968* (Bloomington: Indiana Univ. Press, 1970) [Z8230/ B8/1970], which also includes an extensive explication index for individual poems.

THEODORE DREISER (1871–1945)

Many people who have written about Theodore Dreiser write more gracefully than he, but few reveal more of the man than he does himself in such exercises in self-examination as *Hey Rub-a-Dub-Dub: A Book of the Mystery and Wonder and Terror of Life* (New York: Boni and Liveright, 1920) [PS3507/R55H4]; *A Book about Myself* (New York: Boni and Liveright, 1922) [PS3507/ R55Z5]; and *Moods, Cadenced and Declaimed* (New York: Boni and Liveright, 1926) [PS3507/R55M6]. Revealing also is what is reported, based on conversations with him, in H. L. Mencken, *A Book of Prefaces* (New York: Knopf, 1917) [PS121/M4]. Every student of Dreiser is grateful for Robert H. Elias's bibliographical essay in *Sixteen Modern American Authors: A Survey in Research and Criticism* (see "Bibliographies"), which is reprinted in part, and expanded, from the bibliographical section of the "emended edition" of his 1949 standard critical biography, *Theodore Dreiser: Apostle of Nature** (Ithaca, N.Y.: Cornell Univ. Press, 1970) [PS3507/R55Z63/1970]. Elias has also edited *Letters of Theodore Dreiser: A Selection*, 3 vols. (Philadelphia: Univ. of Pennsylvania Press, 1950) [PR3507/R55Z54], which reveals the novelist's relationships to and opinions of his literary contemporaries and his conception of the role of the literary artist. W. A. Swanburg, *Dreiser* (New York: Scribner's, 1965) [PS3507/R55Z84] is a massively informative biography—but one that attempts little critical examination of the writings. Brief, but critically sound, is Philip L. Gerber, *Theodore Dreiser** (New York: Twayne, 1964) [PS3507/ R55Z636].

F. O. Matthiessen, *Theodore Dreiser* (New York: Sloane, 1949) [PS3507/R55Z7] is a discriminating critical study. Ellen Moers, *Two Dreisers* (New York: Viking, 1969) [PS3507/R55Z74], though primarily an examination of how *Sister Carrie* and *An American*

Tragedy were written, contains fresh critical insights. Charles Child Walcutt, "The Three Stages of Dreiser's Naturalism," *PMLA*, 55 (March 1944), 266–89, expanded in *American Literary Naturalism: A Divided Stream* (Minneapolis: Univ. of Minnesota Press, 1956) [PS379/W28], has become a landmark in Dreiser criticism. Much is said in praise of the novelist in James T. Farrell, *The League of Frightened Philistines, and Other Papers* (New York: Vanguard, 1945) [PS3511/A738A16/1945]. Dreiser has been judiciously attacked in Lionel Trilling, "Dreiser and the Liberal Mind," *Nation*, 162 (20 April 1946), 466–72, which was revised and expanded as "Reality in America," in Trilling's *The Liberal Imagination: Essays on Literature and Society** (New York: Viking, 1950) [PS3539/R5L5]. The most complete sympathetic critical study is Robert Penn Warren, *Homage to Theodore Dreiser, August 27, 1871–December 28, 1945, on the Centennial of His Birth* (New York: Random House, 1971) [PS3507/R55Z86], which is one novelist's close examination of the writings of another novelist—and a book in which it has been said that Dreiser finds his ideal reader at last.

Alfred Kazin and Charles Shapiro, eds., *The Stature of Theodore Dreiser: A Critical Survey of the Man and His Work** (Bloomington: Indiana Univ. Press, 1955) [PS3507/R55Z64] and John Lydenberg, ed., *Dreiser: A Collection of Critical Essays** (Englewood Cliffs, N.J.: Prentice-Hall, 1971) [PS3507/R55Z67] are gatherings of miscellaneous sound criticism. Dreiser's reputation in the nation's review media can be traced in Jack Salzman, ed., *Theodore Dreiser: The Critical Reception* (New York: David Lewis, 1972) [PS3507/R552818].

T. S. ELIOT (1888–1965)

Because he was a superior writer, Eliot has attracted many superior commentators. There is as yet, however, no satisfactory biography: several reminiscent accounts reveal more of the "reminiscer" than of the person remembered. Herbert Howarth, *Notes on Some Figures behind T. S. Eliot* (Boston: Houghton Mifflin, 1964) [PS3509/L43Z684] is a useful survey of the background against which the poet can be viewed. Better as biography is Bernard Bergonzi, *T. S. Eliot** (New York: Macmillan, 1972) [PS3509/L43Z643], an unpretentious and judicious book that reveals Eliot's public life and contains sensitive interpretations of his writings. Richard March and Thurairajah Tambimuttu, eds., *T. S. Eliot: a Symposium from Conrad Aiken [and Others]* (London: Editions Poetry, 1948) [PS3509/L43Z73] contains six essays that recall incidents in the poet's life. The winter 1966 issue of *Sewanee Review* contains other reminiscent essays by people who knew Eliot, notably Herbert Read, "T. S. E.: A Memoir," (74:31–57).

Eliot's poetry is gathered in two volumes: *Collected Poems, 1909–1962* (New York: Harcourt, Brace & World, 1963) [PS3509/L43A17] and *Poems Written in Early Youth** (London: Faber and Faber, 1967) [PS3509/L43A17/1967]. A convenient single-volume, but incomplete, collection is *Complete Poems and Plays* (New York: Harcourt, Brace, 1952) [PS3509/L43/1952]. His criticism has not been collected, but much of the best of it appears in *Selected Essays: New Edition* (New York: Harcourt, Brace, 1950) [PN511/E443/1950].

Most students find F. O. Matthiessen, *The Achievement of T. S. Eliot: An Essay on the Nature of Poetry,** 2d ed. (New York: Oxford Univ. Press, 1947) [PS3509/L43Z74/1947] the most satisfying introduction to Eliot's poetry and plays; it was reissued in 1958 with additional chapters by C. L. Barber on the later writings [PS3509/L43Z74/1958]. Also usually considered indispensable are Elizabeth Drew, *T. S. Eliot: The Design of His Poetry** (New York: Scribner's, 1949) [PS3509/L43Z67]; Helen Gardner, *The Art of T. S. Eliot** (New York: Dutton, 1949) [PS3509/L43Z675]; D. E. S. Maxwell, *The Poetry of T. S. Eliot** (London: Routledge & Paul, 1952) [PS3509/L43Z78/1952]; Grover Smith, *T. S. Eliot's Poetry and Plays: A Study of Sources and Meaning** (Chicago: Univ. of Chicago Press, 1956) [PS3509/L43Z868]; Hugh Kenner, *The Invisible Poet: T. S. Eliot** (New York: McDowell, Obolensky, 1959) [PS3509/L43Z69]; and Leonard Unger, *T. S. Eliot: Movements and Patterns** (Minneapolis: Univ. of Minnesota Press, 1966) [PS3509/L43Z884]. George Williamson, *A Reader's Guide to T. S. Eliot: A Poem-by-Poem Analysis** (New York: Noonday, 1953) [PS3509/L43Z898] offers useful explications. Useful brief introductions include Philip Headings, *T. S. Eliot** (New York: Twayne, 1964) [PS3509/L43Z682] and Neville Braybrooke, *T. S. Eliot: A Critical Essay** (Grand Rapids, Mich.: Eerdmans, 1967) [PS3509/

L43Z6444]. A lively French estimate is Georges Cattaui, *T. S. Eliot** (London: Merlin, 1966) [PS3509/L43Z648].

Much perceptive criticism of Eliot's work has appeared in periodicals: Edmund Wilson, "The Poetry of Drouth," *Dial,* 73 (December 1922), 611–616, is expanded in *Axel's Castle: A Study in the Literature of 1870–1930* (New York: Scribner's, 1931) [PN771/W55]; R. P. Blackmur, "T. S. Eliot," *Hound & Horn,* 1 (May 1920), 187–213, but see also his *The Double Agent* (New York: Arrow, 1935) [PS324/B6] and "In the Hope of Straightening Things Out," *Kenyon Review,* 13 (Spring 1951), 300–14; Theodore Spencer, "The Poetry of T. S. Eliot," *Atlantic Monthly,* 151 (January 1933), 60–68; Cleanth Brooks, "The Waste Land: An Analysis," *Southern Review,* 1 (Autumn 1936), 568–83, revised as "The Waste Land: Critique of the Myth," in *Modern Poetry and the Tradition* (Chapel Hill: Univ. of North Carolina Press, 1939) [PN1136/B75]; C. L. Barber, "T. S. Eliot after Strange Gods," *Southern Review,* 6 (May 1940), 387–416; F. R. Leavis, "Eliot's Later Poetry," *Scrutiny,* 11 (Summer 1942), 65–67; Rene Wellek, "The Criticism of T. S. Eliot," *Sewanee Review,* 64 (Summer 1956), 398–430; Austin Warren, "T. S. Eliot's Literary Criticism," *Sewanee Review,* 74 (Winter 1966), 272–92; and Donald Gallup, "T. S. Eliot and Ezra Pound," *Atlantic Monthly,* 225 (January 1970), 48–62.

Antagonistic to Eliot are Ernest Sutherland Bates, "T. S. Eliot: Middle Class Laureate," *Modern Monthly,* 7 (February 1933), 17–24; Yvor Winters, "T. S. Eliot: The Illusion of Reaction," *Kenyon Review,* 3 (Winter, Spring 1941), 7–30, 221–39, reprinted in his *The Anatomy of Nonsense* (Norfolk, Conn.: New Directions, 1943) [PN99/U5W5]; Rossell Hope Robbins, *The T. S. Eliot Myth* (New York: Schuman, 1951) [PS3509/L43Z825]; and Karl Shapiro, *In Defense of Ignorance* (New York: Random House, 1960) [PS3509/L43Z74]. For a balanced consideration of Eliot's achievement and shortcomings, see Stanley Edgar Hyman, *The Armed Vision: A Study in Modern Literary Criticism** (New York: Harper, 1951) [PN771/Z2].

Collections of essays include B. Rajan, ed., *T. S. Eliot: A Study of His Writings by Several Hands* (New York: Funk & Wagnalls, 1948) [PS3509/L32Z82]; Hugh Kenner, ed., *T. S. Eliot: A Collection of Critical Essays** (Englewood Cliffs, N.J.: Prentice-Hall, 1962) [PS3509/L43Z6913]; and A. Walton Litz, ed., *Eliot in His*

Time: Essays on the Occasion of the Fiftieth Anniversary of The Waste Land (Princeton: Princeton Univ. Press, 1973) [PS3509/L43W3687].

Collections that speak of Eliot's best known poem are C. B. Cox and Arnold P. Hinchliffe, eds., *T. S. Eliot, The Waste Land: A Casebook* (London: Macmillan, 1968) [PS3509/L43W364] and, especially valuable, Jay Martin, ed., *A Collection of Critical Essays on The Waste Land** (Englewood Cliffs, N.J.: Prentice-Hall, 1968) [PS3509/L43W369]. Valerie Eliot, ed., *The Waste Land: A Facsimile and Transcript of the Original Drafts Including the Annotations of Ezra Pound* (New York: Harcourt, Brace, Jovanovich, 1971) [PS3509/L43W3/1971b] presents an almost unique opportunity to watch a poet as his poem progresses through many drafts, revisions, and deletions.

RALPH WALDO EMERSON (1803–1882)

Definitive editions of *The Collected Works of Ralph Waldo Emerson* in twelve volumes and of *The Journals and Miscellaneous Notebooks of Ralph Waldo Emerson* in sixteen volumes are being published by the Belknap Press of Harvard University Press; its three-volume edition of *The Early Lectures of Ralph Waldo Emerson,* edited by Stephen E. Whicher, Robert E. Spiller, and Wallace E. Williams, is now complete [PS1602/W5]. Ralph Leslie Rusk, ed., *The Letters of Ralph Waldo Emerson,* 6 vols. (New York: Columbia Univ. Press, 1939) [PS1631/A3/1939] can be supplemented by Joseph Slater, ed., *The Correspondence of Emerson and Carlyle* (New York: Columbia Univ. Press, 1964) [PS1631/A35C3]. A facsimile edition of *Nature** (1836) with an introduction by Warner Berthoff is available (San Francisco: Chandler, 1968) [PS1620/A1]; see also Merton M. Sealts, Jr., and Alfred R. Ferguson, eds., *Emerson's Nature—Origin, Growth, Meaning* (New York and Toronto: Dodd, Mead, 1969) [PS1613/S4], which contains the text, sources, and criticisms of Emerson's first volume. A facsimile edition of *Essays* (1841) and *Essays: Second Series* (1844) in one volume, with an introduction by Morse Peckham, is also available (Columbus, Ohio: Merrill, 1969) [PS1608/A1/1969]. Of the many reprints or collections of Emerson's writings, the following can be especially useful: Mark Van Doren, ed., *The Portable Emerson** (New York: Viking, 1946) [PS1602/V28]; Alfred Kazin and Daniel Aaron, eds., *Emerson: A Modern Anthology* (Boston: Houghton Mifflin, 1959) [PS1603/K33]; Robert E. Spiller, ed., *Selected Essays, Lectures and Poems of Ralph Waldo Emerson* (New York: Washington Square, 1965) [PS1603/S6]; and Reginald Cook, ed., *Ralph Waldo Emerson: Selected Prose and Poetry*, 2d ed. (New York: Holt, Rinehart & Winston, 1969) [PS1602/C6/1969].

The definitive biography is Ralph Leslie Rusk, *The Life of Ralph Waldo Emerson* (New York: Scribner's, 1949) [PS1631/R78], which should, however, be supplemented by Stephen E. Whicher, *Freedom and Fate: An Inner Life of Ralph Waldo Emerson** (Philadelphia: Univ. of Pennsylvania Press, 1953) [PS1631/W5], which many think is the single best introduction to Emerson's life and works. Edward Wagenknecht, *Ralph Waldo Emerson: Portrait of a Balanced Soul* (New York: Oxford Univ. Press, 1974) [PS1631/W3] is a sound introduction to Emerson's person and contains an extensive bibliography. Frederick Ives Carpenter, *Emerson Handbook* (New York: Hendricks, 1953) [PS1631/C34] offers a well-ordered survey of Emerson's principal ideas and of his reputation. Van Wyck Brooks, *The Life of Emerson* (New York: Dutton, 1932) [PS1631/B65], written in large part "in Emerson's own words," is informative and readable. Edward Waldo Emerson, *Emerson in Concord: A Memoir Written for the "Social Circle" in Concord, Mass.* (Boston: Houghton Mifflin, 1889) [PS1631/E5] contains a son's informal recollections of his father. Frank B. Sanborn, *The Personality of Emerson* (Boston: C. E. Goodspeed, 1903) [PS1631/S35] includes reminiscences of Emerson by a man who knew him. Bliss Perry, *Emerson Today* (Princeton: Princeton Univ. Press, 1931) [PS1638/P4] is a brief but brilliant classic characterization. Josephine Miles, *Ralph Waldo Emerson** (Minneapolis: Univ. of Minnesota Press, 1964) [PS1634/M55] is a sensitive and sound brief introduction.

Phases of Emerson's life are examined in Arthur C. McGiffert, Jr., *Young Emerson Speaks* (Boston: Houghton Mifflin, 1938) [BX9843/E487Y6], which tells of his experience as a young clergyman; Townsend Scudder, III, *The Lonely Wayfaring Man: Emerson and Some Englishmen* (New York: Oxford Univ. Press, 1936) [PS1631/S43], which tells of his early experiences abroad;

and Henry F. Pommer, *Emerson's First Marriage* (Carbondale: Southern Illinois Univ. Press, 1967) [PS1632/P6] and Edith W. Gregg, ed., *One First Love: The Letters of Ellen Louisa Tucker to Ralph Waldo Emerson* (Cambridge: Belknap Press of Harvard Univ. Press, 1962) [PS1632/G3], each of which tells of an early great crisis in Emerson's life. The extensiveness of his activity as a lecturer is glimpsed in William Charvat, ed., *Emerson's American Lecture Engagements: A Chronological List* (New York: New York Public Library, 1961) [PS1631/C4]. Joel Porte, *Emerson and Thoreau: Transcendentalists in Conflict* (Middleton, Conn.: Wesleyan Univ. Press, 1966) [PS1631/P6] tells of Emerson's relationship with his quirky neighbor.

Emerson's protean thought has been discovered to arise from several sources. Lawrence Buell, *Literary Transcendentalism: Style and Vision in the American Renaissance* (Ithaca, N.Y.: Cornell Univ. Press, 1973) [PS217/T7B8] explains contemporary intellectual currents that derived from or influenced Emerson; this volume can be helpfully supplemented by Perry Miller, ed., *The Transcendentalists: An Anthology* (Cambridge: Harvard Univ. Press, 1950) [B905/M5], a generous collection of expressions of currents of thought in early nineteenth-century New England. Perry Miller, "From Edwards to Emerson," *New England Quarterly*, 13 (December 1940), 589–613, reprinted with an important corrective headnote in Miller's *Errand into the Wilderness** (Cambridge: Belknap Press of Harvard Univ. Press, 1956) [E169/1/M628], finds Emerson's philosophy to have sprung from native roots.

But other roots have also been suggested. J. S. Harrison, *The Teachers of Emerson* (New York: Sturgis & Walton, 1910) [PS1636/H3] finds them in Platonism and Neoplatonism. John P. Pritchard, *Return to the Fountains: Some Classical Sources of American Criticism* (Durham, N.C.: Duke Univ. Press, 1932) [PN99/U5P7] underlines the influence of the classics. Frederick I. Carpenter, *Emerson and Asia* (Cambridge: Harvard Univ. Press, 1930) [PS1642/A7C3] and Arthur E. Christy, *The Orient in American Transcendentalism* (New York: Columbia Univ. Press, 1932) [B905/C5] explains the influences of oriental thought on Emerson. Henry A. Pochmann, *German Culture in America: Philosophical and Literary Influences, 1600–1900* (Madison: Univ. of Wisconsin Press, 1957) [E169/1/P596] devotes a large section of this book to the importance of German thought to Emerson. William M. Wynkoop, *Three Children of the Universe: Emerson's View of Shakespeare, Bacon, and Milton* (The Hague: Mouton, 1966) [PS1631/W9/1966] points to some of the important influences on Emerson that derived from English literature. Roland Lee, "Emerson through Kierkegaard," *Journal of English Literary History*, 26 (September 1957), 229–48, places Emerson among the early existentialists.

After Stephen E. Whicher's *Freedom and Fate*, mentioned above, perhaps the finest critical introduction to Emerson is in Book One of F. O. Matthiessen, *American Renaissance: Art and Expression in the Age of Emerson and Whitman** (New York: Oxford Univ. Press, 1941) [PS201/M3]. Other influential critiques are found in John Jay Chapman, *Emerson and Other Essays*, rev. ed. (New York: Moffat, Yard, 1909) [PN511/C4/1909], which defends Emerson as a literary artist more proficient in prose than in verse; Sherman Paul, *Emerson's Angle of Vision: Man and Nature in American Experience* (Cambridge: Harvard Univ. Press, 1952) [PS1638/P3], which suggests that Emerson's simple confidence in poetic harmonies stood in the way of his complete utilization of symbolic possibilities; Vivian Hopkins, *Spires of Form: A Study of Emerson's Aesthetic Theory* (Cambridge: Harvard Univ. Press, 1951) [PS1642/A3H6]; and Jonathan Bishop, *Emerson on the Soul* (Cambridge: Harvard Univ. Press, 1964) [PS1642/R4B5], an important, fresh explanation of how Emerson transformed organic unity into rhythms, metaphors, and tone. For a noteworthy, fresh, and perceptive view, see Tony Tanner, "The Unconquered Eye and the Enchanted Circle," in *The Reign of Wonder: Naivety and Reality in American Literature* (Cambridge, Eng.: Cambridge Univ. Press, 1965) [PS88/T25].

Emerson's verse has been critically reevaluated in Hyatt H. Waggoner, *Emerson the Poet* (Princeton: Princeton Univ. Press, 1974) [PS1638/W3]. Nelson F. Adkins, "Emerson and the Bardic Tradition," *PMLA*, 63 (June 1948), 662–77 is an important earlier explanation of Emerson's concept of what poetry should be. For a discussion of Emerson's poetry in relation to its time and to native traditions, see Roy Harvey Pearce, *The Continuity of American Poetry* (Princeton: Princeton Univ. Press, 1961) [PS303/P4] and especially Hyatt H. Waggoner, *American Poetry from the Puritans to the Present* (Boston: Houghton Mifflin, 1968) [PS303/W3], which finds Emerson "the central figure in American poetry, essential both as spokesman and catalyst."

Not every critic has approved of Emerson. Among those who have most effectively attacked him are Yvor Winters, *Maule's Curse: Seven Studies in the History of American Obscurantism* (Norfolk, Conn.: New Directions, 1938) [PS201/W5], who upbraids him as "a fraud and a sentimentalist." Henry Bamford Parkes, *The Pragmatic Test* (San Francisco: Colt, 1941) [B29/P33] argues that the whole tendency of Emerson's philosophy "was to destroy the tradition in which virtues such as his own could be cultivated." Quentin Anderson, *The Imperial Self: An Essay in American Literary and Cultural History** (New York: Knopf, 1971) [PS201/A5] argues that Emerson's dependence on inspiration set a faulty pattern for later writers.

Useful gatherings of critical essays include Milton R. Konvitz, ed., *The Recognition of Ralph Waldo Emerson: Selected Criticism since 1837* (Ann Arbor: Univ. of Michigan Press, 1972) [PS1638/K8]; Carl Bode, ed., *Ralph Waldo Emerson: A Profile** (New York: Hill and Wang, 1968) [PS1631/B57]; and Milton R. Konvitz and Stephen E. Whicher, eds., *Emerson: A Collection of Critical Essays** (Englewood Cliffs, N.J.: Prentice-Hall, 1962) [PS1631/K6].

WILLIAM FAULKNER (1897–1962)

A good deal more has been written about Faulkner than he in his novels ever wrote. His life has been massively detailed in Joseph Blotner, *Faulkner: A Biography,* 2 vols. (New York: Random House, 1974) [PS3511/A86Z625]. Much of the earlier writing about Faulkner was marred by errors of fact, but, combining a fine critical sense with excellent biography, Michael Millgate, *The Achievement of William Faulkner** (New York: Random House, 1966) [PS3511/A894/1966a] is the best short reliable biographical study and, with Cleanth Brooks, *William Faulkner: The Yoknapatawpha Country** (New Haven: Yale Univ. Press, 1963) [PS3511/A86Z64], offers the most comprehensive criticism of his works. John Faulkner, *My Brother Bill: An Affectionate Reminiscence** (New York: Trident, 1963) [PS3511/A86Z783] and Murry C. Falkner,

The Falkners of Mississippi: A Memoir (Baton Rouge: Louisiana State Univ. Press, 1967) [PS3511/A86Z7832] are reminiscent family accounts by the novelist's younger brothers. John B. Cullen, in collaboration with Floyd C. Watkins, *Old Times in the Faulkner Country* (Chapel Hill: Univ. of North Carolina Press, 1961) [PS3511/A86Z78] collects reminiscent anecdotes from one of Faulkner's hunting companions. James W. Webb and A. Wigfall Green, eds., *William Faulkner of Oxford** (Baton Rouge: Louisiana State Univ. Press, 1965) [PS3511/A86Z9854] contains anecdotes remembered by Faulkner's fellow townsmen. The most satisfying brief introduction to the life and writings is Michael Millgate, *William Faulkner*, rev. ed. (New York: Barnes & Noble, 1966) [PS3511/A86Z895/1966]. Some find useful Lewis Leary, *William Faulkner of Yoknapatawpha County* (New York: Crowell, 1973) [PS3511/A86Z875].

Faulkner is intimately revealed in interviews with students in Joseph L. Fant and Robert Ashley, eds., *Faulkner at West Point** (New York: Random House, 1964) [PS3511/A86Z54]; Frederick L. Gwynn and Joseph L. Blotner, eds., *Faulkner at the University: Class Conferences at the University of Virginia, 1957–1958** (Charlottesville: Univ. Press of Virginia, 1959) [PS3511/A86Z53]; and Robert A. Helliffe, ed., *Faulkner at Nagano* (Tokyo: Kenkyusha, 1956) [PS3511/A86Z523], which contains transcripts of interviews and seminar discussions during Faulkner's 1955 visit to Japan. James E. Meriwether and Michael Millgate, eds., *Lion in the Garden* (New York: Random House, 1966) [PS3511/L564], is another revealing collection of interviews. But Faulkner is perhaps most intimately displayed in his correspondence gathered in Malcolm Cowley, *The Faulkner-Cowley File: Letters and Memories, 1944–1962* (New York: Viking, 1966) [PS3511/A86Z77], which contains information about the man and his writings, some of which had been previously used in Malcolm Cowley, ed., *The Portable Faulkner** (New York: Viking, 1946), revised and expanded in 1967 [PS3511/A86A6/1968].

Besides the books by Millgate and Brooks, mentioned above, helpful critical estimates are also found in Irving Howe, *William Faulkner: A Critical Study*, 2d ed. (New York: Vintage, 1952) [PS3511/A86Z84/1962]; Olga W. Vickery, *The Novels of William Faulkner: A Critical Introduction*, rev. ed. (Baton Rouge: Louisiana

State Univ. Press, 1964) [PS3511/A86Z98/1964], a pioneering work that linked structure to meaning in the major novels; Hyatt H. Waggoner, *William Faulkner: From Jefferson to the World** (Lexington: Univ. of Kentucky Press, 1959) [PS3511/A86/Z985]; Peter Swiggart, *The Art of Faulkner's Novels* (Austin: Univ. of Texas Press, 1962) [PS3511/A86Z974], which clarified notions about Faulkner's art that other critics had not made plain; Richard P. Adams, *Faulkner: Myth and Motion* (Princeton: Princeton Univ. Press, 1968) [PS3511/A86Z556], which examined the "astonishing amount and varieties of cultural materials" behind Faulkner's writing; Joseph W. Reed, Jr., *Faulkner's Narrative* (New Haven: Yale Univ. Press, 1973) [PS3511/A86Z947]; and Panthea Reid Broughton, *William Faulkner: The Abstract and the Actual* (Baton Rouge: Louisiana State Univ. Press, 1974) [PS3511/A86Z644].

Useful brief critical introductions, which, however, must be checked for accuracy, are Lawrance Thompson, *William Faulkner: An Introduction and Interpretation,* 2d ed. (New York: Holt, Rinehart & Winston, 1967) [PS3511/A86Z977/1967] and Frederick J. Hoffman, *Willam Faulkner** (New York: Twayne, 1961) [PS3511/A86Z79]. Edmond L. Volpe, ed., *A Reader's Guide to William Faulkner** (New York: Farrar, Straus, 1964) [PS3511/A86Z983] and Dorothy Tuck, ed., *Crowell's Handbook of Faulkner** (New York: Crowell, 1964) [PS3511/A86Z978] provide excellent guides to the novelist's themes, plots, and characters.

Frederick J. Hoffman and Olga W. Vickery, eds., *William Faulkner: Three Decades of Criticism** (East Lansing: Michigan State Univ. Press, 1960) [PS3511/A86Z8] contains twenty-four critical essays, unequal in quality; those by Conrad Aiken, Alfred Kazin, and Robert Penn Warren are, however, important critical statements about the man and his methods. See also Linda W. Wagner, ed., *William Faulkner: Four Decades of Criticism* (East Lansing: Michigan State Univ. Press, 1973) [PS3511/A86Z9852] and Dean W. Schmitter, ed., *William Faulkner: A Collection of Criticism* (New York: McGraw-Hill, 1973) [PS3511/A86Z966]. More carefully selective is Robert Penn Warren, ed., *Faulkner: A Collection of Critical Essays** (Englewood Cliffs, N.J.: Prentice-Hall, 1966) [PS3511/A86Z9853].

John Bassett, comp., *William Faulkner: An Annotated Checklist of Criticism* (New York: Lewis, 1972) [Z8288/B38] can be consulted for guidance through the barrage of critical studies on Faulkner that, since the mid-1940s, have quickened literary debate in this country and abroad.

F. SCOTT FITZGERALD (1896–1940)

Fitzgerald's short, unhappy life and large literary achievement are best revealed in Arthur Mizener, *The Far Side of Paradise: A Biography of F. Scott Fitzgerald,** rev. ed. (Boston: Houghton Mifflin, 1965) [PS3511/I9Z7]. His personal life is set forth in sympathetic detail in Sheila Graham, *Beloved Infidel** (New York: Holt, 1958) [PN4874/G67A3], an autobiographical account by a person who was close to Fitzgerald in his later years; Nancy Milford, *Zelda: A Biography** (New York: Harper & Row, 1970) [PS3511/I9234Z8/1970], which speaks sensitively of the novelist's wife; Budd Schulberg, *The Disenchanted* (New York: Random House, 1950) [PZ3/S38585D1], a fictionalized account of Fitzgerald's years in Hollywood; and especially Andrew W. Turnbull, *Scott Fitzgerald* (New York: Scribner's, 1962) [PS3511/I9Z88], an intimate and often moving portrait of a man whom the author, as a boy, had known well and had admired. Tony Buttitta, *After the Good Gay Times, Asheville—Summer of '35: A Season with F. Scott Fitzgerald* (New York: Viking, 1974) [PS3511/Z9Z572] contains equally compelling informal reminiscences of a later period.

Reminiscent accounts by expatriate friends include Morley Callaghan, *That Summer in Paris* (New York: Coward-McCann, 1964) [PS3505/A4342Z52]; Ernest Hemingway, *A Movable Feast** (New York: Scribner's, 1964) [PS3515/E37Z525]; and John Dos Passos, *The Best Times: An Informal Memoir* (New York: New American Library, 1966) [PS3507/0743Z49]. Further biographical detail is found in Andrew W. Turnbull, ed., *The Letters of F. Scott Fitzgerald* (New York: Scribner's, 1963) [PS3511/I9Z54]; John Kuehl and Jackson R. Bryer, eds., *Dear Scott/Dear Max—The Fitzgerald-Perkins Correspondence* (New York: Scribner's, 1971) [PS3511/I9Z556], which contains letters to and from his editor at Scribner's; and Matthew J. Bruccoli, ed., *As Ever, Scott Fitz–: Letters between F. Scott Fitzgerald and His Literary Agent Harold Ober—1919–1940* (Philadelphia: Lippincott, 1972) [PS3511/I9Z554].

Although interest in Fitzgerald's life often seems to overshadow interest in his writings, there are excellent critical studies, the most persuasive of which are James E. Miller, Jr., *F. Scott Fitzgerald: His Art and Technique** (New York: New York Univ. Press, 1964) [PS3511/I9Z688]; Robert D. Lehan, *F. Scott Fitzgerald and the Craft of Fiction* (Carbondale: Southern Illinois Univ. Press, 1966) [PS3511/I9Z68]; and Robert Sklar, *F. Scott Fitzgerald: The Last Laocoön** (New York: Oxford Univ. Press, 1967) [PS3511/I9Z86]. Excellent brief studies are Charles E. Shain, *F. Scott Fitzgerald* (Minneapolis: Univ. of Minnesota Press, 1961) [PS3511/I9Z85]; Kenneth Eble, *F. Scott Fitzgerald** (New York: Twayne, 1963) [PS3511/I9Z6]; and, perhaps best, Milton Hindus, *F. Scott Fitzgerald: An Introduction and Interpretation** (New York: Barnes & Noble, 1968) [PS3511/I9Z66/1968].

Noteworthy essays include Maxwell Geismar, "F. Scott Fitzgerald: Orestes at the Ritz," in *The Last of the Provincials: The American Novel, 1915–1925: H. L. Mencken, Sinclair Lewis, Willa Cather, Sherwood Anderson, F. Scott Fitzgerald*, 2d ed. (Boston: Houghton Mifflin, 1949) [PS379/G36/1949]; Charles Weir, Jr., "An Invite with Gilded Edges," *Virginia Quarterly Review*, 20 (April 1944), 100–13; William Troy, "Scott Fitzgerald: The Anatomy of Failure," *Accent*, 6 (August 1945), 56–60; John W. Aldridge, "Fitzgerald: The Horror and the Vision of Paradise," in *After the Lost Generation: A Critical Study of the Writers of Two Wars* (New York: McGraw-Hill, 1951) [PS379/A5]; the brief but brilliant commentary in Richard Chase, *The American Novel and Its Tradition** (Garden City, N.Y.: Doubleday, 1957) [PS371/C5]; Wright Morris, "The Function of Nostalgia: F. Scott Fitzgerald," in *The Territory Ahead** (New York: Harcourt, Brace, 1962) [PS88/M6], in which one novelist talks of another; and James Gindin, "Gods and Fathers in Scott Fitzgerald's Novels," *Modern Language Quarterly*, 30 (March 1969), 64–85.

Volumes of collected criticism include Alfred Kazin, ed., *F. Scott Fitzgerald: The Man and His Work** (Cleveland: World, 1951) [PS3511/I9Z67]; Arthur Mizener, ed., *F. Scott Fitzgerald: A Collection of Critical Essays** (Englewood Cliffs, N.J.: Prentice-Hall, 1963) [PS3511/I9Z698]; Ernest H. Lockridge, ed., *Twentieth Century Interpretations of "The Great Gatsby"** (Englewood Cliffs, N.J.: Prentice-Hall, 1968) [PS3511/I9G86]; and Matthew J. Bruccoli and Jackson R. Bryer, eds., *F. Scott Fitzgerald in His Own Time:*

A Miscellany* (Kent, Ohio: Kent State Univ. Press, 1971) [Z8396/ 3/B76]. Bryer's *The Critical Reputation of F. Scott Fitzgerald: A Bibliographical Study* (Hamden, Conn.: Archon, 1967) [PS3511. I9Z57] is an indispensable guide to the criticism.

BENJAMIN FRANKLIN (1706–1790)

The text of Franklin's writings, formerly somewhat unkempt, is now being made neatly available. The Yale University Press is issuing a complete edition in twenty-five volumes of *The Papers of Benjamin Franklin,* edited by Leonard W. Labaree and others, and has issued *The Autobiography of Benjamin Franklin* (1967) [E302/ 6/F7A2/1967], printed from the original manuscript and edited for the general reader. Claude-Anne Lopez and Willard B. Trask, eds., *The Bagatelles from Passy . . . Text and Facsimile* (New York: Eakins, 1967) [PS750/B3/1967] presents an accurate text of Franklin's later essays.

The most complete modern biography is Carl Van Doren, *Benjamin Franklin* (New York: Viking, 1938) [E302/6/F8V32], but see also Paul Leicester Ford, *The Many-Sided Franklin* (New York: Century, 1899) [E302/6/F8F7] and Alfred Owen Aldridge, *Benjamin Franklin: Philosopher and Man* (Philadelphia: Lippincott, 1965) [E302/6/F8A46]. Bruce Ingham Granger, *Benjamin Franklin: An American Man of Letters* (Ithaca, N.Y.: Cornell Univ. Press, 1964) [PS751/G7] focuses on the writer rather than on the public person; see also Lewis Leary, "Benjamin Franklin and the Requirements of Literature in America," in *Soundings: Some Early American Writers* (Athens: Univ. of Georgia Press, 1975) [PS193/ L4]. Richard E. Amacher, ed., *Franklin's Wit and Folly: The Bagatelles* (New Brunswick, N.J.: Rutgers Univ. Press, 1953) [PS750/B3/1953] contains lively critical comment. Max Hall, *Benjamin Franklin and Polly Baker: The History of a Literary Deception* (Chapel Hill: Univ. of North Carolina Press, 1960) [PN171/F7B3] is a delightful account of the origin and fate of "The Speech of Polly Baker," which has been called America's first short story. Robert F. Sayre, *The Examined Self: Benjamin Franklin, Henry Adams, Henry James* (Princeton: Princeton Univ. Press, 1964) [CT25/S2] compares Franklin's *Autobiography* to those of Henry Adams and Henry James.

Among the few articles that speak effectively of Franklin's literary activities are Paul Elmer More, "Franklin in Literature," *Independent*, 60 (11 January 1906), 98–104; Max Farrand, "Benjamin Franklin Memoirs," *Huntington Library Bulletin*, 10 (October 1936), 48–78; Louis B. Wright, "Franklin's Legacy to the Gilded Age," *Virginia Quarterly Review*, 22 (March 1946), 268–79; Lewis Leary, "Joseph Dennie on Benjamin Franklin: A Note on Early American Literary Criticism," *Pennsylvania Magazine of History and Biography*, 72 (July 1948), 240–46; Jesse Bier, "Franklin's *Autobiography*: Benchmark of American Literature," *Western Humanities Review*, 12 (Winter 1958), 57–65; David Levin, "The *Autobiography of Benjamin Franklin*: The Puritan Experimenter in Life and Art," *Yale Review*, 53 (Winter 1964), 258–75; J. A. Leo Lemay, "Franklin and the Autobiography: An Essay on Recent Scholarship," *Eighteenth-Century Studies*, 1 (1967), 185–211; and M. L. Ross, "Poor Richard and *Playboy*: Brothers under the Flesh," *Colorado Quarterly*, 25 (Spring 1967), 355–60. Chester E. Jorgenson and Frank Luther Mott, eds., *Benjamin Franklin: Representative Selections* (1936) has been reprinted with a useful updated bibliography (New York: American Book Company, 1951) [PS745/A3/M7].

ROBERT FROST (1874–1963)

The writings in verse of Robert Frost are effectively collected in Edward Connery Lathem, ed., *The Poetry of Robert Frost* (New York: Holt, Rinehart & Winston, 1969) [PS3511/R94/1969], which combines Frost's eleven books into one volume. *Selected Poems of Robert Frost** (New York: Holt, Rinehart & Winston, 1963) [PS3511/R94A6/1963] was prepared by Frost and contains some revised versions of his poems. Some of his prose writings appear in Edward Connery Lathem and Lawrance Thompson, eds., *Robert Frost: Farm Poultryman* (Hanover, N.H.: Dartmouth Publications, 1963) [PS3511/R94A16], which brings together articles by Frost that appeared in poultry journals, and Hyde Cox and Edward Connery Lathem, eds., *Selected Prose of Robert Frost** (New York: Holt, Rinehart & Winston, 1966) [PS3511/R94A16/1966]. His letters are gathered in Louis Untermeyer, ed., *The Letters of Robert*

Frost to Louis Untermeyer (New York: Holt, Rinehart & Winston, 1963) [PS3511/R94Z53]; Margaret Bartlett Anderson, ed., *Selected Letters of Robert Frost* (New York: Holt, Rinehart & Winston, 1964) [PS3511/R94Z52/1964]; and Andre Grade, ed., *Family Letters of Robert and Elinor Frost* (Albany: State Univ. of New York Press, 1972) [PS3511/R94Z53/1972]. Interviews with Frost are recorded in Daniel Smythe, *Robert Frost Speaks* (New York: Twayne, 1964) (PS3511/R94Z924]; Louis Mertins, ed., *Robert Frost: Life and Talks–Walking* (Norman: Univ. of Oklahoma Press, 1965) [PS3511/R94Z786]; and Edward Connery Lathem, *Interviews with Robert Frost* (New York: Holt, Rinehart & Winston, 1966) [PS3511/R94I55].

The "official" biography, planned for three volumes—of which two have appeared—is Lawrance Thompson, *Robert Frost: The Early Years, 1874–1915* (New York: Holt, Rinehart & Winston, 1966) [PS3511/R94Z953] and *Robert Frost: The Years of Triumph, 1915–1938* (New York: Holt, Rinehart, & Winston, 1970) [PS3511/R94Z954]. Elizabeth Shepley Sergeant, *Robert Frost: The Trial by Existence* (New York: Holt, Rinehart & Winston, 1960) [PS3511/R94Z92] is judiciously appreciative rather than analytical. Sidney Cox, *A Swinger of Birches: A Portrait of Robert Frost** (New York: New York Univ. Press, 1957) [PR3511/R94Z59], with an introduction by Frost, is a kindly tribute to the "wisest man I know." Dependable brief biographies are Philip L. Gerber, *Robert Frost* (New York: Twayne, 1966) [PS3511/R94Z66] and Lawrance Thompson, *Robert Frost,** rev. ed. (Minneapolis: Univ. of Minnesota Press, 1967) [PS3511/R94Z95].

There is no scarcity of critical studies. Lawrance Thompson, *Fire and Ice: The Art and Thought of Robert Frost* (New York: Holt, 1942) [PS3511/R94Z93] is a basic introduction to the poet's methods and thought. Reginald Cook, *The Dimensions of Robert Frost* (New York: Rinehart, 1958) [PS3511/R94Z585] is a quietly appreciative critical estimate directed toward revealing interrelationships between the man and the poetry. George W. Nitchie, *Human Values in Poetry of Robert Frost: A Study of a Poet's Convictions* (Durham, N.C.: Duke Univ. Press, 1960) [PS3511/R94Z85/1960] examines the ethical and philosophical premises behind the poems. John F. Lynen, *The Pastoral Art of Robert Frost* (New Haven: Yale Univ. Press, 1960) [PS3511/R94Z77] may place too much emphasis on the poet's rusticity, but it contains sound readings of some of the most familiar poems. Of major importance are Radcliffe Squires, *The Major Themes of Robert Frost** (Ann Arbor: Univ. of Michigan Press, 1963) [PS3511/R94Z925] and especially Reuben Brower, *The Poetry of Robert Frost: Constellations of Intention** (New York: Oxford Univ. Press, 1963) [PS3511/R94Z556], a sensitive and critical close examination of Frost's poems which concludes that he belongs "in the constellation of Yeats and Wallace Stevens," an estimate that some have considered to be somewhat too generous.

Reginald L. Cook, "Emerson and Frost: A Parallel of Seers," *New England Quarterly*, 31 (June 1958), 200–17, and A. S. Ryan, "Frost and Emerson: Voice and Vision," *Massachusetts Review*, 1 (October 1959), 5–23, explain the poet's native roots, as does Mark Van Doren, "Robert Frost's America," *Atlantic Monthly*, 187 (June 1951), 32–34. Randall Jarrell, "The Other Mr. Frost," in *Poetry and the Age* (New York: Knopf, 1953) [PN127/J3] suggests that even in Frost's country poems there is a dark and brooding quality. Lionel Trilling, "A Speech on Robert Frost: A Cultural Episode," *Partisan Review*, 26 (Summer 1959), 445–52, found him "a terrifying poet," with undertones of dark gloom. James Dickey, "Robert Frost, Man and Myth," *Atlantic Monthly*, 218 (November 1966), 53–56, points to two aspects of Frost, one "a remnant of the frontier and the Thoreauistic virtues of shrewd Yankeedom," the other, of a person driven by "paranoic esteem with attendant devils of humiliation, jealousy, and frustration." Archibald MacLeish, *A Continuing Journey* (Boston: Houghton Mifflin, 1968) [PS3535/A27C69] characterizes the later Frost as "a rebellious, brave, magnificent, far-wandering, unbowed old man, who made his finest music out of manhood and met the furies on their own dark ground."

Some earlier critics had found serious faults in Frost. See R. P. Blackmur, "The Instincts of a Bard," *Nation*, 142 (24 June 1936), 819, which describes him as an unskilled craftsman; Malcolm Cowley, "Frost: A Dissenting Opinion," *New Republic*, 111 (11, 18 September 1944), 312–13, 345–47, which finds him provincial; and Yvor Winters, "Robert Frost: Or the Spiritual Drifter as Poet," *Sewanee Review*, 56 (Autumn 1948), 564–96, which discovers inadequacies in thought and expression in most of Frost's writing.

Other essays, mostly favorable, are gathered in Richard Thornton, ed., *Recognition of Robert Frost* (New York: Holt, 1937) [PS3511/R94Z4], which contains criticism from 1913–1937; Robert A. Greenberg and James G. Hepburn, eds., *Robert Frost: An Introduction* (New York: Holt, Rinehart, & Winston, 1961) [PS3511/R94Z7], which contains poems, reviews, and criticism; and James M. Cox, ed., *Robert Frost: A Collection of Critical Essays** (Englewood Cliffs, N.J.: Prentice-Hall, 1962) [PS3511/R94Z588].

NATHANIEL HAWTHORNE (1804–1864)

The Centenary Edition of the Works of Nathaniel Hawthorne is currently being issued by the Ohio State University Press. Hawthorne's letters, never completely brought together, are also being collected for publication. Randall Stewart, ed., *The American Notebooks of Nathaniel Hawthorne* (New Haven: Yale Univ. Press, 1932) [PS1865/A1/1932] and Stewart's *The English Notebooks of Nathaniel Hawthorne* (New York: Modern Language Association of America; London: Oxford Univ. Press, 1941) [PS1881/A43] are impeccably edited from manuscript sources.

Perhaps because Hawthorne was a modest man, the best writing about him has been modest also. Randall Stewart, *Nathaniel Hawthorne: A Biography* (New Haven: Yale Univ. Press, 1948) [PS1881/S67] is a model of what a life study can be; not overcrowded with unnecessary fact or shackled with superfluous annotation, it reveals a writer who "touched his times at point after point with an admonitory finger," pointing toward the shared fallibility of all mankind. Henry James, *Hawthorne* (London: Macmillan, 1879) [PS1881/J3/1879] is valuable as much for what it reveals of the man who wrote it as for what it says so well of the man it was about. Like Newton Arvin, *Hawthorne* (Boston: Little, Brown, 1929) [PS1881/A7] and Mark Van Doren, *Nathaniel Hawthorne* (New York: Sloane, 1949) [PS1881/V3], James's study is more valuable for critical insight than for biographical information. Edward Wagenknecht, *Nathaniel Hawthorne: Man and Writer* (New York: Oxford Univ. Press, 1961) [PS1881/W3], hardly critical at all, supplies answers to the question, "What was he like, this man Hawthorne, whose eyes gaze upon us so quizzically from the old portraits?" The most useful brief survey is Arlin Turner, *Nathaniel Hawthorne: An Introduction and Interpretation** (New York: Barnes & Noble, 1961) [PS1881/T8].

The ideas that underlie Hawthorne's fiction are summarized with authority in Austin Warren, ed., *Nathaniel Hawthorne: Representative Selections* (New York: American Book Company, 1934) [PS1852/W3] and are discriminatingly discussed in F. O. Matthiessen, *American Renaissance: Art and Expression in the Age of Emerson and Whitman** (New York: Oxford Univ. Press, 1941) [PS201/M3]. Insights into Hawthorne's techniques are well set forth in Leland Schubert, *Hawthorne, the Artist: Fine-Art Devices in Fiction* (Chapel Hill: Univ. of North Carolina Press, 1944) [PS1888/S45], which traces rhythmic motifs and the use of color and sound in Hawthorne's fiction; to many, Schubert seems particularly helpful in discussion of the short stories. Richard Harter Fogle, *Hawthorne's Fiction: The Light and the Dark*, rev. ed. (Norman: Univ. of Oklahoma Press, 1964) [PS1888/F6] and its supplementary volume, *Hawthorne's Imagery: The Proper Light and Shadow in the Major Romances* (Norman: Univ. of Oklahoma Press, 1949) [PS1888/F62] contain perhaps the best revelation of Hawthorne's use of such antitheses as light versus darkness, appearance versus reality. Hyatt H. Waggoner, *Hawthorne: A Critical Study*, rev. ed. (Cambridge: Belknap Press of Harvard Univ. Press, 1963) [PS1888/W3/1963] points to important recurring images that suggest or reinforce Hawthorne's subtle meanings. Millicent Bell, *Hawthorne's View of the Artist* (Albany: State Univ. of New York Press, 1962) [PS1888/B4] surveys Hawthorne's critical theories in their relation to romanticism; it should be read in conjunction with Marjorie Elder, *Nathaniel Hawthorne: Transcendental Symbolist** (Athens: Ohio Univ. Press, 1969) [PS1888/E4], which finds Bell failing to present clearly Hawthorne's concept of the artist. Roy R. Male, *Hawthorne's Tragic Vision** (Austin: Univ. of Texas Press, 1957) [PS1888/M3] sees Hawthorne's attitudes toward the conflict between aspirations of the individual and what life requires of him as part of the climate of opinion of his time. Frederick Crews, *The Sins of the Fathers: Hawthorne's Psychological Themes** (New York: Oxford Univ. Press, 1966) [PS1881/C7/1966] uses Hawthorne's writings as the basis for a Freudian analysis of the man.

Primary for an understanding of one of Hawthorne's major

antitheses are Donald A. Ringe, "Hawthorne's Psychology of Head and Heart," *PMLA,* 65 (March 1950), 120–32, and Nina Baym, "The Head, the Heart, and the Unpardonable Sin," *New England Quarterly,* 40 (March 1967), 31–47. Other influential essays have been Walter Blair, "Color, Light and Shadow in Hawthorne's Fiction," *New England Quarterly,* 15 (March 1942), 74–91; Philip Rahv, "The Dark Lady of Salem," *Partisan Review,* 8 (September-October 1941), 262–81, reprinted in *Literature and the Sixth Sense* (Boston: Houghton Mifflin, 1969) [PN761/R26]; and Charles Child Walcutt, "*The Scarlet Letter* and Its Modern Critics," *Nineteenth-Century Fiction,* 7 (March 1953), 251–64, which surveys the amazing variety of interpretations of that novel. Important critical statements are also found in Marius Bewley, *The Complex Fate: Hawthorne, Henry James and Some Other American Writers* (London: Chatto & Windus, 1951) [PS323/B4]; R. W. B. Lewis, *The American Adam: Innocence, Tragedy, and Tradition in the Nineteenth Century** (Chicago: Univ. of Chicago Press, 1955) [PS201/L4]; and Harry Levin, *The Power of Blackness: Hawthorne, Poe, Melville* (New York: Knopf, 1958) [PS1888/L4]. Lionel Trilling, "Our Hawthorne," *Partisan Review,* 21 (Summer 1964), 329–51, is reprinted in Roy Harvey Pearce, ed., *Hawthorne Centenary Essays* (Columbus: Ohio State Univ. Press, 1964) [PS1888/P4], a collection of critical estimates that every student would find it profitable to consult.

The decline of Hawthorne's creative powers in his later years is solidly reviewed in Edward H. Davidson, *Hawthorne's Last Phase* (New Haven: Yale Univ. Press, 1949) [PS1882/D37] and with suggestive speculation in Rudolph Von Abele, *The Death of the Artist: A Study of Hawthorne's Disintegration* (The Hague: Martinus Nijhoff, 1955) [PS1881/V6].

Additional critical commentary is gathered in A. N. Kaul, ed., *Hawthorne: A Collection of Critical Essays** (Englewood Cliffs, N.J.: Prentice-Hall, 1965) [PS1881/K3/1966]. B. Bernard Cohen, *The Recognition of Nathaniel Hawthorne: Selected Criticism since 1828* (Ann Arbor: Univ. of Michigan Press, 1969) [PS1881/C56] contains the often-quoted appraisals by Edgar Allan Poe and Herman Melville. For Hawthorne's most read novel, see Seymour L. Gross, ed., *A Scarlet Letter Handbook** (San Francisco: Wadsworth, 1960) [PS1868/G7]; Kenneth S. Lynn, *The Scarlet Letter: Texts, Sources,*

*Criticism** (New York: Harcourt, Brace & World, 1961) [PZ3/ H318Sc94]; John C. Gerber, ed., *Twentieth-Century Interpretations of The Scarlet Letter** (Englewood Cliffs, N.J.: Prentice-Hall, 1968) [PS1868/G38]; and Arlin Turner, *The Merrill Studies in The Scarlet Letter** (Columbus, Ohio: Merrill, 1970) [PS1868/T8].

ERNEST HEMINGWAY (1899–1961)

Hemingway is said not to have liked the explanation of his life and writings contained in Philip Young, *Ernest Hemingway* (New York: Rinehart, 1952) [PS3515/E37Z96], revised and expanded as *Ernest Hemingway: A Reconsideration* (University Park: Pennsylvania State Univ. Press, 1966) [PS3515/E37Z982/1966], which discovers a pattern of movement—from innocence to initiation to acceptance of a restrictive code—both in the novelist's life and in his writings. He preferred Carlos Baker, *Hemingway: The Writer as Artist** (Princeton: Princeton Univ. Press, 1952), revised and enlarged for a fourth edition in 1972 (PS3515/E37Z58/ 1972], a simpler account that focused on Hemingway's writings. After Hemingway's death, Baker was encouraged to write a complete "authorized" biography, *Ernest Hemingway: A Life Story** (New York: Scribner's, 1969) [PS3515/E37Z575/1969], a book noteworthy for its dogged adherence to fact. Charles A. Fenton, *The Apprenticeship of Ernest Hemingway: The Early Years* (New York: Farrar, Straus & Young, 1954) [PS3515/E37Z59] examines the process by which Hemingway transformed a conventional talent into an artistic skill. Reminiscences by Lillian Ross, *Portrait of Hemingway* (New York: Simon and Schuster, 1961) [PS3515/ E37Z77]; Leicester Hemingway, *My Brother, Ernest Hemingway* (Cleveland: World, 1962) [PS3515/E37Z62]; A. E. Hotchner, *Papa Hemingway: A Personal Memoir** (New York: Random House, 1966) [PS3515/E37Z635]; and William Seward, *My Friend Ernest Hemingway: An Affectionate Reminiscence* (South Brunswick, N.Y.: Barnes, 1969) [PS3515/E37Z826] contain interesting anecdotes, but they are colored by extremes of admiration or dislike. The ideas behind the fiction are explicated by Robert O. Stephens, *Hemingway's Nonfiction: The Public Voice* (Chapel Hill: Univ. of North Carolina Press, 1968) [PS3515/E37Z88].

Of first importance as criticism is Richard B. Hovey, *Hemingway: The Inward Terrain* (Seattle: Univ. of Washington Press, 1968) [PS3515/E37Z636], which examines the writings without dependence on the legends that Hemingway and others built up about his life, but which concludes that Hemingway's art did follow patterns dictated by personal tensions. Sound brief critical surveys are Sheridan Baker, *Ernest Hemingway: An Introduction and Interpretation* (New York: Holt, Rinehart & Winston, 1968) [PS3515/E37Z582] and Leo Gurko, *Ernest Hemingway and the Pursuit of Heroism* (New York: Crowell, 1968) [PS3515/E37Z613]. Commentary on his successes and failures are found in Maxwell Geismar, "Ernest Hemingway: You Could Always Come Back," in *Writers in Crisis: The American Novel between Two World Wars* (Boston: Houghton Mifflin, 1942) [PS379/G4]; John W. Aldridge, "Hemingway and the Correlative of Loss," in *After the Lost Generation: A Critical Study of the Writers of Two Wars* (New York: McGraw-Hill, 1951) [PS379/A5]; Cleanth Brooks, "Ernest Hemingway: Man on His Moral Uppers," in *The Hidden God: Studies in Hemingway, Faulkner, Yeats, Eliot, and Warren* (New Haven: Yale Univ. Press, 1963) [PS228/C5B7]; and, perhaps with greatest simplicity, Tony Tanner, "Ernest Hemingway's Unhurried Sensations," in *The Reign of Wonder: Naivety and Reality in American Literature* (Cambridge: Cambridge Univ. Press, 1965) [PS88/T25].

Much of the most perceptive early commentary has appeared in periodicals: Gertrude Stein, "Ernest Hemingway and the Post-War Decade," *Atlantic Monthly*, 152 (August 1933), 197–208; Wyndham Lewis, "The Dumb Ox: A Study of Ernest Hemingway," *American Review*, 6 (June 1934), 289–312; John Beale Bishop, "The Missing All," *Virginia Quarterly Review*, 13 (Winter 1937), 107–121; and Edmund Wilson, "Ernest Hemingway: Bourbon Gauge of Morality," *Atlantic Monthly*, 163 (July 1939), 36–46. Later articles worth examining include Wilbur M. Frohock, "Ernest Hemingway: Violence and Discipline," *Southwest Review*, 32 (Winter, Spring 1947), 89–97, 184–193, reduced and put in larger perspective in W. M. Frohock, *The Novel of Violence in America,** 2d ed. (Dallas: Southern Methodist Univ. Press, 1958) [PS379/F7/1958]; Robert Penn Warren, "Hemingway," *Kenyon Review*, 9 (Winter 1947), 1–28; Ray B. West, "Ernest Hemingway: The Failure of Sensibility," *Sewanee Review*, 53 (Winter 1949), 120–

35; John B. Colvert, "Ernest Hemingway's Mortality in Action," *American Literature*, 27 (November 1955), 372–85; Edwin Fussell, "Hemingway and Mark Twain," *Accent*, 14 (Summer 1954), 199–206; and John Glendenning, "Hemingway's Gods, Dead and Alive," *Texas Studies in Literature and Language*, 3 (1962), 488–502.

Other essays are gathered in John K. M. McCaffery, ed., *Ernest Hemingway, the Man and His Work* (Cleveland: World, 1950) [PS3515/E37Z7]; Carlos Baker, ed., *Hemingway and His Critics: An International Anthology** (New York: Hill and Wang, 1961) [PS3515/E37Z577]; Robert P. Weeks, ed., *Hemingway: A Collection of Critical Essays** (Englewood Cliffs, N.J.: Prentice-Hall, 1962) [PS3515/E37Z94]; and Jackson J. Benson, ed., *The Short Stories of Ernest Hemingway: Critical Essays* (Durham: Duke Univ. Press, 1975) [PS3515/E37/Z8274]. A thorough guide to material is Andre Hanneman, *Ernest Hemingway: A Comprehensive Bibliography* (Princeton: Princeton Univ. Press, 1967) [Z8396/3/H45], for which a supplement will be published.

WILLIAM DEAN HOWELLS (1837–1920)

Howells is a good but not an exciting writer, and people who write about him tend to share his characteristics. Indiana University Press is issuing a selected edition of W. D. Howells, which will include nearly forty volumes and a complete bibliography. His life story is told in Edwin Harrison Cady, *The Road to Realism: The Early Years, 1837–1885, of William Dean Howells* [PS2033/C25] and its sequel, *The Realist at War: The Mature Years, 1885–1920, of William Dean Howells* (Syracuse: Syracuse Univ. Press, 1956, 1958) [PS2033/C23], as well as in Kenneth S. Lynn, *William Dean Howells: An American Life* (New York: Harcourt, Brace, Jovanovich, 1971) [PS2033/L9]. Clara M. Kirk and Rudolf Kirk, *William Dean Howells** (New York: Twayne, 1962) [PS2033/K5] is a reasonable, brief study. Everett Carter, *Howells and the Age of Realism* (Philadelphia: Lippincott, 1954) [PS2033/C3] is an analysis of the era in which the novelist flourished.

Clara Marburg Kirk, *W. D. Howells and the Art of His Times* (New Brunswick, N.J.: Rutgers Univ. Press, 1965) [PS2033/K49] surveys the novelist's view of America in the late nineteenth century.

Henry Nash Smith and William M. Gibson, eds., *Mark Twain-Howells Letters: The Correspondence of Samuel L. Clemens and William Dean Howells, 1872-1910,** 2 vols. (Cambridge: Belknap Press of Harvard Univ. Press, 1961) [PS1331/A3H6] reveals Howells's not always placid but commonsense attitudes toward literature and life. Collections of criticism are Edwin H. Cady and David L. Frazier, eds., *The War of the Critics over William Dean Howells* (Evanston, Ill.: Row, Peterson, 1962) [PS2034/C3] and Kenneth E. Eble, ed., *Howells: A Century of Criticism* (Dallas: Southern Methodist Univ. Press, 1962) [PS2034/E2].

The most insightful critical estimate is Lionel Trilling, "W. D. Howells and the Roots of Modern Taste," *Partisan Review,* 18 (September-October 1951), 516–37, reprinted in Trilling's *The Opposing Self: Nine Essays in Criticism* (New York: Viking, 1955) [PN511/T76]. Two studies by George N. Bennett pay close attention to Howells's artistry, *William Dean Howells: The Development of a Novelist* (Norman: Univ. of Oklahoma Press, 1959) [PS2033/B4] and *The Realism of William Dean Howells* (Nashville: Vanderbilt Univ. Press, 1973) [PS2034/B4].

WASHINGTON IRVING (1783–1859)

Twayne Publishers is completing the twenty-eight-volume edition of *The Complete Works of Washington Irving,* including his journals and letters, which had been begun by the University of Wisconsin Press. Irving's life is recorded in largely undocumented detail by his nephew, Pierre M. Irving, *The Life and Letters of Washington Irving,* 4 vols. (New York: Putnam, 1862–1864) [PS2081/A3].

Although highly regarded in his own lifetime, Irving has not until recently received important attention in our time. Much of the earlier commentary has been more concerned with his life and thought than with his literary accomplishments. George S. Hellman, *Washington Irving, Esquire: Ambassador at Large from the New World to the Old* (New York: Knopf, 1925) [PS2081/H4] is informal and anecdotal. Henry A. Pochmann, ed., *Washington Irving: Representative Selections* (New York: American Book Company, 1934) [PS2053/P6] presents a solid appraisal of Irving's milieu, political opinions, philosophical views, and literary development.

Stanley T. Williams, *The Life of Washington Irving*, 2 vols. (New York: Oxford Univ. Press, 1935) [PS2081/W45] is a valuable and well-documented account, only casually—and then usually acerbically —critical. Edward Wagenknecht, *Washington Irving: Moderation Displayed* (New York: Oxford Univ. Press, 1962) [PS2081/W2] tells a pleasant story of a whimsical man. Van Wyck Brooks, *The World of Washington Irving* (New York: Dutton, 1944) [PS208/ B7], though deriving its title from the period from 1800 to 1840 in which Irving flourished, has less to say of Irving than of his contemporaries. Lewis Leary, *Washington Irving** (Minneapolis: Univ. of Minnesota Press, 1963) [PS2081/L4/1963] is brief and not always commendatory.

Only William L. Hedges, *Washington Irving: An American Study, 1802–1832* (Baltimore: Johns Hopkins Press, 1965) [PS2081/ H35] views Irving at length seriously as an artist, seeing him in relationship to such contemporaries as Edgar Allan Poe and Nathaniel Hawthorne: "The essential characteristic of Irving's stories is that they are told by a man who is not altogether sure of himself. . . . Irving's is a fiction of dreams, fantasies, symbolic projection; it is heavily loaded with imagery functioning as metaphor," yet he showed a way that others would follow.

Irving's importance as an innovator had been suggested by two earlier brief accounts. Though Henry A. Pochmann, "Irving's German Sources in *The Sketch Book*," *Studies in Philology*, 27 (July 1934), 477–507, demonstrates that the plot for "Rip Van Winkle" had been borrowed from abroad, Philip Young, "Fallen From Time: The Mythic Rip Van Winkle," *Kenyon Review*, 22 (August 1960), 547–73, finds the story, whatever its sources, impressively symbolic of the American notion that time can be slept away, so that a man remains a boy who never quite grows up, but remains eternally, in his own mind's eye, "a kid with a dog." Daniel G. Hoffman, *Form and Fable in American Fiction** (New York: Oxford Univ. Press, 1961) [PS377/H6] identifies Ichabod Crane in "The Legend of Sleepy Hollow" as Irving's Connecticut Yankee, a jack of many trades who anticipates Mark Twain's versatile mechanic, and Brom Bones as an anticipation of the rugged frontiersman who outwits the city slicker in thousands of later dime novels and popular magazines.

Irving's activities abroad can best be followed in Stanley T.

Williams, *The Spanish Backgrounds of American Literature*, 2 vols. (New Haven: Yale Univ. Press, 1955) [PS159/S7W5]; Nathalia Wright, *American Novelists in Italy: The Discoverers, Allston to James** (Philadelphia: Univ. of Pennsylvania Press, 1965) [PS377/ W7/1965]; and Walter A. Reichert, *Washington Irving and Germany* (Ann Arbor: Univ. of Michigan Press, 1957) [PS2081/R4]. Ben Harris McClary, ed., *Washington Irving and the House of Murray: Geoffrey Crayon Charms the British, 1817–1856* (Knoxville: Univ. of Tennessee Press, 1969) [PS2081/A3/1969] details Irving's relationships with his English publisher. James T. Callow, *Kindred Spirits: Knickerbocker Writers and American Artists, 1807– 1855* (Chapel Hill: Univ. of North Carolina Press, 1967) [PS255/ N5C3] has things to say of his relationships at home.

Two collections of appraisals, mainly laudatory, have appeared: Ralph Aderman, ed., *Washington Irving Reconsidered: A Symposium* (Hartford, Conn.: Transcendental, 1969) [PS2088/W35] and Andrew B. Myers, ed., *Washington Irving: A Tribute** (Tarrytown, N.Y.: Sleepy Hollow Restorations, 1972) [PS2085/W3/1970].

HENRY JAMES (1843–1916)

The Novels and Tales of Henry James, 26 vols. (New York: Scribner's, 1907–1917) [PS2110/F07] contain important prefaces by the author, which have been collected in R. P. Blackmur, ed., *The Art of the Novel: Critical Prefaces** (New York: Scribner's, 1934) [PS2112/A3/1934]. The edition was reprinted, with additions, as *The Novels and Tales of Henry James*, 35 vols. (London: Macmillan, 1921–1923) [PS2110/F07/1921]. Leon Edel, ed., *The Complete Tales of Henry James*, 12 vols. (Philadelphia: Lippincott, 1962–1965) [PZ3/J234C12] reprints the short stories and novelettes. F. O. Matthiessen and Kenneth B. Murdock, eds., *The Notebooks of Henry James* (New York: Oxford Univ. Press, 1947) [PS2123/ A4]; Leon Edel, ed., *The Complete Plays of Henry James* (Philadelphia: Lippincott, 1949) [PS2111/E4]; and Frederick W. Dupee, ed., *Henry James: Autobiography* (New York: Criterion, 1956) [PS2123/A3] are important primary sources of information on the man and his works. Selected essays are found in Morris Roberts, ed., *The Art of Fiction and Other Essays* (New York: Oxford Univ. Press,

1948) [PN3499/J25]; Leon Edel, ed., *The Future of the Novel: Essays on the Art of Fiction* (New York: Vintage, 1956) [PN3354/ J3]; and Morris Shapira, ed., *Henry James: Selected Literary Criticism* (New York: Horizon, 1964) [PN710/J3/1964]. The first two volumes of a planned four-volume edition are Leon Edel, ed., *Henry James: Letters, 1843–1875* (Cambridge: Belknap Press of Harvard Univ. Press, 1974, 1975) [PS2123/A5/1974].

His life is recorded in almost too much detail in Leon Edel, *Henry James: The Untried Years, 1843–1870* (Philadelphia: Lippincott, 1953) [PS2123/E33], followed by Edel's *Henry James: The Conquest of London, 1870–1881* (1962) [PS2123/E34], *Henry James: The Middle Years, 1882–1895* (1962) [PS2123/E35], *Henry James: The Treacherous Years, 1895–1901* (1969) [PS2123/E36], and *Henry James: The Master, 1901–1916* (1972) [PS2123/E37]. These volumes constitute an indispensable and monumental work, marred only by their author's predilection for psychological analysis. More moderate and consistently dependable approaches will be found in F. W. Dupee, *Henry James** (New York: Sloane, 1951) [PS2123/ D8] or in Joseph Warren Beach, *The Method of Henry James,** rev. ed. (Philadelphia: Saifer, 1954) [PS2124/B4/1954], each of which is modest, compact, and has proved to be durable. Bruce R. McElderry, Jr., *Henry James** (New York: Twayne, 1965) [PS2121/ M26] is another temperate study, with discrete balance between biography and criticism. Lyall H. Powers, *Henry James: An Introduction and Interpretation** (New York: Holt, Rinehart & Winston, 1967) [PS2124/P65] is an extraordinarily good brief account of James's life and writings.

Critical estimates of superior quality are numerous. One of the more recent is Harry T. Moore, *Henry James* (New York: Viking, 1974) [PS2123/M63/1974], containing well-balanced judgments clearly expressed by a leading authority on modern fiction. The question of James's alienation from his homeland is argued in Van Wyck Brooks, *The Pilgrimage of Henry James* (New York: Dutton, 1925) [PS2123/B7], which describes the novelist as unable to come to grips with his native environment, and Pelham Edgar, *Henry James: Man and Author* (Boston: Houghton Mifflin, 1927) [PS2123/ E4/1964], which explains that, having exhausted native materials, James did the sensible thing by moving to Europe, from where he could view America and Americans more objectively. Quentin

Anderson, *The American Henry James* (New Brunswick, N.J.: Rutgers Univ. Press, 1957) [PS2124/A43/1957], a controversial but fascinating book, discovers roots indeed in native soil, finding James's major novels to be fictional representations, sometimes almost allegorical, of his Swedenborgian father's anti-Emersonian transcendentalism.

The novelist's early career is well set forth in Cornelia P. Kelley, *The Early Development of Henry James*, rev. ed. (Urbana: Univ. of Illinois Press, 1930) [PS2123/K4/1965] and is critically reviewed in Richard Poirier, *The Comic Sense of Henry James: A Study of the Early Novels* (London: Chatto & Windus, 1961) [PS2124/P6/1960a]. An authoritative account of the novels of James's later years is F. O. Matthiessen, *Henry James: The Major Phase* (New York: Oxford Univ. Press, 1944) [PS2124/M3], but see also Frederick C. Crews, *The Tragedy of Manners: Moral Drama in the Later Novels of Henry James* (New Haven: Yale Univ. Press, 1957) [PS2124/C7]. Other studies that have proved to be helpful include Elizabeth Stevenson, *The Crooked Corridor: A Study of Henry James* (New York: Macmillan, 1949) [PS2123/S8], which finds the main theme of James's novels to be the conflict between the individual and society; Osborn Andreas, *Henry James and the Expanding Horizon: A Study of the Meaning and Basic Themes of James's Fiction* (Seattle: Univ. of Washington Press, 1948) [PS2124/A5]; Edwin T. Bowden, *The Themes of Henry James: A System of Observation through the Visual Arts* (New Haven: Yale Univ. Press, 1956) [PS2124/B6/1969]; and Robert L. Gale, *The Caught Image: Figurative Language in the Fiction of Henry James* (Chapel Hill: Univ. of North Carolina Press, 1964) [PS2124/G3]. An essential reference book is Oscar Cargill, *The Novels of Henry James* (New York: Macmillan, 1961) [PS2124/C25], which surveys the critical commentary that has been written on each of the important novels.

Much superior criticism is found in essays: Edmund Wilson, "The Ambiguity of Henry James," *Hound & Horn*, 7 (April-June 1934), 385–406, reprinted in *The Triple Thinkers: Ten Essays on Literature* (New York: Harcourt, Brace, 1938) [PN511/W63]; Yvor Winters, "Henry James and the Relation of Morals to Manners," *American Review*, 9 (October 1937), 482–503, reprinted in *In Defense of Reason** (Denver: Swallow, 1947) [PS121/W53]; Jacques Barzun, "James the Melodramatist," *Kenyon Review*, 5

(August 1943), 508–12, reprinted in *The Energies of Art* (New York: Harper, 1962) [PN511/B35]; Marius Bewley, "Appearance and Reality in Henry James," *Scrutiny*, 17 (Summer 1950), 90–114, reprinted with other essays on James in *The Complex Fate: Hawthorne, Henry James, and Some Other American Writers* (London: Chatto and Windus, 1952) [PS323/B4]; R. P. Blackmur, "The Loose and Baggy Monsters of Henry James," *Accent*, 11 (Summer 1951), 129–46, reprinted in *The Lion and the Honeycomb: Essays in Solicitude and Critique* (New York: Harcourt, Brace, 1955) [PS121/B59]; and Morton Dauwen Zabel, "Henry James: The Art of Life," in *Craft and Character: Texts, Methods, and Vocation in Modern Fiction* (New York: Viking, 1957) [PR823/Z3]. F. R. Leavis, *The Great Tradition: George Eliot, Henry James, Joseph Conrad** (London: Chatto and Windus, 1948) [PR873/L4/1948a] places James among English novelists; Leavis is corrected by Richard Chase, *The American Novel and Its Tradition** (Garden City: Doubleday, 1957) [PS371/C5].

Other essays often consulted are Joseph J. Firebaugh, "The Pragmatism of Henry James," *Virginia Quarterly Review*, 27 (Summer 1951), 419–35; Priscilla Gibson, "The Uses of James's Imagery: Drama through Metaphor," *PMLA*, 69 (December 1954), 1076–84; Alfred R. Ferguson, "The Triple Quest of Henry James: Fame, Art, and Fiction," *American Literature*, 27 (January 1956), 475–98; Rene Wellek, "Henry James's Literary Theory and Criticism," *American Literature*, 30 (November 1958), 293–301; Viola Hopkins, "Visual Art Devices and Parallels in the Fiction of Henry James," *PMLA*, 76 (December 1961), 561–74; and Frederick J. Hoffman, "Freedom and Conscious Form: Henry James and the American Self," *Virginia Quarterly Review*, 35 (Spring 1961), 184–97. A delightful spoof of James's style and method is James Thurber, "Onward and Upward through the Arts: The Wings of Henry James," *New Yorker*, 35 (7 November 1959), 184–97.

Gatherings of essays include F. W. Dupee, ed., *The Questions of Henry James: A Collection of Critical Essays* (New York: Holt, 1945) [PS2124/D8]; Naomi Lebowitz, ed., *Discussions of Henry James* (Boston: Heath, 1962) [PS2124/L351]; Leon Edel, ed., *Henry James: A Collection of Critical Essays** (Englewood Cliffs, N.J.: Prentice-Hall, 1963) [PS2124/E38]; Roger Gard, ed., *Henry James: The Critical Heritage* (New York: Barnes and Noble, 1968)

[PS2124/G35]; and Tony Tanner, ed., *Henry James** (Nashville: Aurora, 1970) [PS2124/T3/1970].

Essays on the novels sometimes considered James's best are found in Peter Buitenhuis, ed., *Twentieth-Century Interpretations: The Portrait of a Lady: A Collection of Critical Essays** (Englewood Cliffs, N.J.: Prentice-Hall, 1968) [PS2116/P63B8]; Albert E. Stone, Jr., ed., *Twentieth-Century Interpretations of The Ambassadors** (Englewood Cliffs, N.J.: Prentice-Hall, 1969) [PS2116/A53S8]; see also, Gerald Willen, ed., *A Casebook on Henry James's The Turn of the Screw** (New York: Crowell, 1960) [PS2116/T84], which contains fifteen important critical essays, hardly one of which agrees with any of the others.

HERMAN MELVILLE (1819–1891)

The Writings of Herman Melville, in fifteen volumes, are being issued jointly by Northwestern University Press and the Newberry Library. Merrell R. Davis and William H. Gilman, eds., *The Letters of Herman Melville* (New Haven: Yale Univ. Press, 1960) [PS2387/A57] contains all of Melville's important letters. Letters to or about him are found in Eleanor Melville Metcalf, *Herman Melville: Cycle and Epicycle* (Cambridge: Harvard Univ. Press, 1953) [PS2386/M46]. The texts of Melville's public lectures, largely drawn from newspaper accounts, are given in Merton M. Sealts, Jr., *Melville as Lecturer* (Cambridge: Harvard Univ. Press, 1957) [PS2386/S4].

Jay Leyda, *The Melville Log: A Documentary Life of Herman Melville, 1819–1891,* 2 vols. (New York: Harcourt, Brace, 1951) [PS2386/L4] presents extracts from letters, newspapers, book reviews, and ship logs to provide "the largest possible quantity of materials" and so "give each reader the opportunity to be his own biographer of Herman Melville." Leon Howard, *Herman Melville: A Biography** (Berkeley: Univ. of California Press, 1951) [PS2386/ H6], using Leyda's *Log* as an important source, gives a narrative account of Melville's life that is a masterwork of concision and good sense. William H. Gilman, *Melville's Early Life and Redburn* (New York: New York Univ. Press, 1951) [PS2386/G46] and Perry Miller, *The Raven and the Whale: The War of Words and Wits in* *the Era of Poe and Melville* (New York: Harcourt, Brace, 1956) [PS74/M5] have instructive things to say about Melville's apprenticeship and early writing years. Tyrus Hillway, *Herman Melville** (New York: Twayne, 1963) [PS2386/H5] is a dependable introductory survey of Melville's life and works.

Of the many critical accounts of Melville's writings, three are likely to be preferred. William Ellery Sedgwick, *Melville: The Tragedy of Mind* (Cambridge: Harvard Univ. Press, 1944) [PS2387/S4] is a durable and comprehensive study that suggests that too much thinking finally led to Melville's decline as an artist. Newton Arvin, *Herman Melville* (New York: Sloane, 1950) [PS2386/Z7/1950], marred only by a tendency toward Freudian analysis, is probably the most brilliant book written about Melville, particularly in the treatment of *Moby-Dick*, finding in that novel four levels of meaning: the literal, psychological, moral, and mythic. Warner Berthoff, *The Example of Herman Melville** (Princeton: Princeton Univ. Press, 1962) [PS2386/B4] may be the most satisfactory single introductory account. It examines Melville's fiction as fiction, not as a series of philosophical or moral exercises or as indexes to the character or neuroses of the writer; yet it recognizes "a continuous imaginative presence and energy sustaining . . . and positively generating them." Another useful and straightforward account is Charles Roberts Anderson, *Melville in the South Seas** (New York: Columbia Univ. Press, 1939) [PS2386/A6/1939a], which examines the sources in other men's writings of much of Melville's lore of tropical adventure.

Melville's roving, adventurous mind has attracted critics often as adventuresome and deep-diving as he. Richard Chase, *Herman Melville: A Critical Study* (New York: Macmillan, 1949) [PS2386/C5] suggests that all Melville's novels adumbrate a cultural-historical myth of a fall and then a search for what had been lost by that fall by protagonists who are part Oedipus and part Prometheus—and who usually fail. Lawrance Thompson, *Melville's Quarrel with God* (Princeton: Princeton Univ. Press, 1952) [PS2388/R4T5] finds Melville a blasphemer unable to speak directly of his disbelief and thereby forced to express it indirectly through parable or symbol. James Baird, *Ishmael* (Baltimore: Johns Hopkins Press, 1956) [PN56/P7B3] is a Jungian study of Melville as a maker of myths. H. Bruce Franklin, *The Wake of the Gods: Melville's Mythology**

(Stanford: Stanford Univ. Press, 1953) [PS2388/M9F7] is a compelling explanation of how Melville used myths that had been already created by other men. Merlin Bowen, *The Long Encounter: Self and Experience in the Writings of Herman Melville** (Chicago: Univ. of Chicago Press, 1960) [PS2387/B6/1960] finds in the major works a single individual pitted against a basically hostile universe. Edgar A. Dryden, *Melville's Thematics of Form: The Great Art of Telling the Truth* (Baltimore: Johns Hopkins Press, 1968) [PS2397/D7] has been admired, particularly for its treatment of the shorter tales. Martin Leonard Pops, *The Melville Archetype* (Kent, Ohio: Kent State Univ. Press, 1970) [PS2387/P6] purports to be a study of Melville's "quest for the sacred," but it contains, nonetheless, enlivening close readings of much of his fiction. John D. Seelye, *Melville: the Ironic Diagram* (Evanston, Ill.: Northwestern Univ. Press, 1970) [PS2387/S43], reaching for less, accomplishes more in its focus on matters of form and structure. William R. Dillingham, *An Artist in the Rigging: The Early Work of Herman Melville* (Athens: Univ. of Georgia Press, 1972) [PS2387/D5] traces basic ideas in the early novels.

Howard P. Vincent, *The Trying Out of Moby-Dick** (Boston: Houghton Mifflin, 1949) [PS2384/M62V5] discusses the sources, composition, and meaning of that novel. Charles Olson, *Call Me Ishmael** (New York: Reynal & Hitchcock, 1947) [PS2384/M6204] contains a poet's individualistic commentary, with emphasis on the influence of Shakespeare on Melville's writing. Of primary importance is George R. Stewart, "The Two Moby Dicks," *American Literature*, 25 (January 1954), 417–48, which explains that Melville began to write one book, in one mode, and then, when part way through, changed to another, and then ingeniously patched to join the two parts. Willie T. Weathers, "Moby Dick and the Nineteenth-Century Scene," *Texas Studies in Literature and Language*, 1 (Winter 1960), 477–501 finds contemporary political analogues in the novel.

Tyrus Hillway and Luther S. Mansfield, eds., *Moby-Dick Centennial Essays* (Dallas: Southern Methodist Univ. Press, 1953) [PS2384/M62H4]; Howard P. Vincent, ed., *The Merrill Studies in Moby-Dick** (Columbus, Ohio: Merrill, 1969) [PS2384/M62V49/1969]; and Hershel Parker and Harrison Hayford, eds., *Moby-Dick as Doubloon: Essays and Extracts, 1851–1970** (New

York: Norton, 1970) [PS2384/M6] are generous collections of much of the better criticism written about Melville's most famous book. Also useful for text and commentary is Harrison Hayford and Hershel Parker, eds., *Moby-Dick: An Authoritative Text, Reviews and Letters by Melville, Analogues and Sources, Criticism** (New York: Norton, 1967) [PS2384/M6/1967].

Richard Harter Fogle, *Melville's Shorter Tales* (Norman: Univ. of Oklahoma Press, 1960) [PS2387/F6] is comprehensive and dependable. For individual tales, see Haskell S. Springer, ed., *The Merrill Studies in Billy Budd** (Columbus, Ohio: Merrill, 1970) [PS2384/B7S6]; Harrison Hayford and Merton M. Sealts, Jr., eds., *Billy Budd, Sailor (An Inside Narrative): Reading Text and Genetic Text, Edited from the Manuscript, with Introduction and Notes** (Chicago: Univ. of Chicago Press, 1962) [PS2384/B5/1962]; William T. Stafford, ed., *Melville's Billy Budd and the Critics*, 2d ed. (San Francisco: Wadsworth, 1968) [PS2384/B7S8]; Seymour L. Gross, ed., *A Benito Cereno Handbook* (Belmont, Ca.: Wadsworth, 1965) [PS2384/B42G7]; and Howard P. Vincent, ed., *Bartleby the Scrivener: A Symposium* (Kent, Ohio: Kent State Univ. Press, 1960) [PS2384/B28B3].

Robert Penn Warren, ed., *Selected Poems of Herman Melville: A Reader's Edition* (New York: Random House, 1970) [PS2382/W3/1971] contains a perceptive introductory essay. Thoughtful and comprehensive examinations of Melville's poetry can be found in three essays in *Tulane Studies in English* by Richard Harter Fogle: "Melville's *Clarel*: Doubt and Belief," 10 (1960), 101–16; "Themes in Melville's Later Poems," 11 (1961), 65–85; and "Melville's Poetry," 12 (1962), 81–86.

James E. Miller, Jr., *A Reader's Guide to Herman Melville** (New York: Farrar, Straus, and Cudahy, 1962) [PS2387/M5] and Howard P. Vincent, *The Merrill Guide to Herman Melville* (Columbus, Ohio: Merrill, 1969) [PS2386/V5] are indispensable introductory guides. Other critical commentary is collected in Richard Chase, ed., *Melville: A Collection of Critical Essays** (Englewood Cliffs, N.J.: Prentice-Hall, 1962) [PS2387/C45] and Hershel Parker, ed., *The Recognition of Herman Melville: Selected Criticism since 1846** (Ann Arbor: Univ. of Michigan Press, 1967) [PS2387/P3].

EUGENE O'NEILL (1888–1953)

A complete and dependable biography is Arthur and Barbara Gelb, *O'Neill** (New York: Harper, 1962) [PS3529/N5Z653]. Louis Sheaffer, *O'Neill: Son and Playwright* (Boston: Little, Brown, 1968) [PS3529/N5Z798], and Sheaffer's companion volume, *O'Neill: Son and Artist* (Boston: Little, Brown, 1973) [PS3529/ N5Z797], offer an exhaustive account of O'Neill's life and work, review all the significant criticism on his plays, and include extensive annotated bibliographies; though not explicitly Freudian studies, they examine the sublimation of O'Neill's family conflicts in his plays. Doris Alexander, *The Tempering of Eugene O'Neill* (New York: Harcourt, Brace, 1962) [PS3529/N5Z556] is a scholarly account of the playwright's career to 1920.

Croswell Bowen, *The Curse of the Misbegotten: A Tale of the House of O'Neill* (New York: McGraw-Hill, 1959) [PS3529/ N5Z573] is a revelation of family life as reported by O'Neill's second son, Shane. Agnes Boulton, *Part of a Long Story* (Garden City, New York: Doubleday, 1958) [PS3529/N5Z57] is the story of life with O'Neill as told by his second wife. Frederick I. Carpenter, *Eugene O'Neill** (New York: Twayne, 1964) [PS3529/N5Z578] is a biographical account to which is added a useful survey of the major plays. Jordan Y. Miller, *Eugene O'Neill and the American Critics: A Summary and Bibliographical Checklist* (Hamden, Conn.: Archon, 1962) [Z8644/5/M5] contains a biographical summary, a chronological account of the playwright's activities, and a brief description of each of the plays and of its reception. But perhaps the best introduction to O'Neill's life and writings is Clifford Leech, *Eugene O'Neill* (New York: Grove, 1963) [PS3529/N5Z684/ 1963], a temperate, well-informed, and judicious estimate.

For criticism, John Henry Raleigh, *The Plays of Eugene O'Neill** (Carbondale: Southern Illinois Univ. Press, 1965) [PS3529/ N5Z79] is valuable for its treatment of the plays as literature rather than as dramaturgy. Sophus Keith Winther, *Eugene O'Neill: A Critical Study*, 2d ed. (New York: Russell & Russell, 1961) [PS3529/N5Z9/1961] speaks of the significance of the playwright's thought in relation to the thought of his time. Other significant critical studies include Edwin A. Engel, *The Haunted Heroes of Eugene O'Neill* (Cambridge: Harvard Univ. Press, 1953) [PS3529/ N5Z63], in which each play is carefully analyzed; Doris V. Falk, *Eugene O'Neill and the Tragic Tension: An Interpretive Study of the Plays** (New Brunswick, N.J.: Rutgers Univ. Press, 1958) [PS3529/N5Z64], which points out psychological patterns in the plays and sees O'Neill as a precursor of much modern psychoanalytic theory; and Travis Bogard, *Contour in Time: The Plays of Eugene O'Neill* (New York: Oxford Univ. Press, 1972) [PS3529/ N5Z568], which examines the playwright as an autobiographer who "used the stage as his mirror," so that the sum of his work reveals his own life story. Timo Tiusanen, *O'Neill's Scenic Images* (Princeton: Princeton Univ. Press, 1968) [PS3529/N5Z86] deals not only with the playwright as writer but also with the stage effects that contribute to the total impact and ultimate importance of his work; see also Egil Törngvist, *A Drama in Souls: Studies in O'Neill's Supernaturalistic Technique* (Stockholm: Almqvist & Wiksell, 1968) [PS3529/N5Z87], which extends much the same thesis about the importance of stage effects. Not to be overlooked is John Gassner, *Eugene O'Neill* (Minneapolis: Univ. of Minnesota Press, 1965) [PS3529/N5Z647/1965], a brief and unpretentious, but reliable, critical introduction.

Essays that have been influential include Joseph Wood Krutch, "O'Neill's Tragic Sense," *American Scholar*, 16 (Summer 1947), 283–90 (see also his *The American Drama Since 1918: An Informal History*, rev. ed. (New York: Braziller, 1957) [PS351/K7/1957] for a more extended treatment); Robert Brustein, "America's New Culture Hero: Feelings without Words," *Commentary*, 25 (February 1958), 123–29 (see also his *The Theatre of Revolt: An Approach to the Modern Drama** (Boston: Little, Brown, 1964) [PN2189/ B7]); and Arthur H. Nethercot, "The Psychoanalyzing of Eugene O'Neill," *Modern Drama*, 3 (December 1960, February 1961), 242–56, 357–72. Other essays and reviews are gathered in Oscar Cargill and others, eds., *O'Neill and His Plays: Four Decades of Criticism* (New York: New York Univ. Press, 1961) [PS3529/N5Z576]; John Gassner, ed., *O'Neill: A Collection of Critical Essays* (Englewood Cliffs, N.J.: Prentice-Hall, 1964) [PS3529/N5Z648]; Jordan Y. Miller, ed., *Playwright's Progress: O'Neill and the Critics** (Chicago: Scott, Foresman, 1965) [PS3529/N5Z73]; and John

Henry Raleigh, *Twentieth-Century Interpretations of The Iceman Cometh: A Collection of Critical Essays** (Englewood Cliffs, N.J.: Prentice-Hall, 1968) [PS3529/N5Z73].

EDGAR ALLAN POE (1809–1849)

Much of the most perceptive criticism of Poe has been written by other poets: by W. H. Auden in his introduction to his *Edgar Allan Poe: Selected Poetry and Prose* (New York: Rinehart, 1950) [PS2602/A8]; by T. S. Eliot, *From Poe to Valéry* (New York: Harcourt, Brace, 1948) [PS2636/E4/1949], reprinted in *Hudson Review*, 2 (Autumn 1949), 263–74; by Richard Wilbur in his introduction to his selection of Poe's poems, *Poe** (New York: Dell, 1959) [PS2605/A1/1959]; but especially by Allen Tate, "Our Cousin, Mr. Poe," *Partisan Review*, 16 (December 1949), 1207–19, and Tate's "The Angelic Imagination: Poe and the Power of Words," *Kenyon Review*, 14 (Summer 1952), 455–75, both reprinted in Tate's *The Forlorn Demon: Didactic and Critical Essays* (Chicago: Regnery, 1953) [PN37/T28]. Hervey Allen, *Israfel: The Life and Times of Edgar Allan Poe*, 2 vols. (New York: Doran, 1926) [PS2631/A7] is a leisurely and affectionate fellow poet's defense of Poe's shortcomings as man and writer. Daniel Hoffman, *Poe Poe Poe Poe Poe Poe Poe** (Garden City: Doubleday, 1972) [PS2638/H57] is an impressionistic but insightful examination of the many facets of Poe, written by an admiring convert who himself alternates volumes of criticism with volumes of poetry.

There is no completely satisfactory biography. The most detailed is Arthur Hobson Quinn, *Edgar Allan Poe: A Critical Biography* (New York: Appleton-Century, 1941) [PS2631/Q5], which is not critical at all. Joseph Wood Krutch, *Edgar Allan Poe: A Study in Genius* (New York: Knopf, 1926) [PS2638/K7] contains brilliant critical insights based on an assumption that Poe was sexually impotent. N. Bryllion Fagin, *The Histrionic Mr. Poe* (Baltimore: Johns Hopkins Univ. Press, 1949) [PS2631/F3] explains the poet as a frustrated actor. Marie Bonaparte's influential Freudian study, *Edgar Poe: Étude psychoanalytique* (Paris: Denoël et Steele, 1933) [PS2631/B6], translated by John Rodker as *The Life and Words of Edgar Allan Poe: A Psycho-Analytic Interpretation* (London:

Imago, 1949) [PS2631/B62], finds Poe's writings colored by "intense emotional fixations and painful infantile experiences." Vincent Buranelli, *Edgar Allan Poe** (New York: Twayne, 1961) [PS2631/ B82] is misleadingly extravagant in praise. More dependable, though uncritical, is Edward Wagenknecht, *Edgar Allan Poe: The Man behind the Legend* (New York: Oxford Univ. Press, 1963) [PS2631/ W3], a pleasantly readable examination of Poe's character and personality. Some, however, find that John Ward Ostrom, ed., *The Letters of Edgar Allan Poe*, 2 vols. (Cambridge: Harvard Univ. Press, 1948) [PS2631/A374] provides better testimony to Poe's mercurial personality than any of the formal biographies.

Perhaps the best critical introduction is Patrick F. Quinn, *The French Face of Edgar Poe** (Carbondale: Southern Illinois Univ. Press, 1957) [PS2638/Q5], which, though its primary focus is on the response to Poe in France, provides sound interpretations of the principal writings. Edward H. Davidson, *Poe: A Critical Study* (Cambridge: Belknap Press of Harvard Univ. Press, 1957) [PS2638/ D3] studies Poe against a background of intellectual and aesthetic history; its first chapter, "The Necessary Demon: The Poetry of Youth," is especially useful. Not to be overlooked is W. C. Brownell's chapter on Poe in *American Prose Masters* (New York: Scribner's, 1909) [PS362/B7], which discovers Poe to be more artisan than artist. Yvor Winters, "Edgar Allan Poe: A Crisis in the History of American Obscurantism," *American Literature*, 8 (January 1937), 379–401, reprinted in Winters's *Maule's Curse: Seven Studies in the History of American Obscurantism* (Norfolk, Conn.: New Directions, 1938) [PS201/W5], speaks of Poe as a confused poet of the second class.

Robert D. Jacobs, *Poe: Journalist & Critic* (Baton Rouge: Louisiana State Univ. Press, 1969) [PS2638/J3] constitutes a major contribution toward understanding Poe's career as a magazinist and the sources of his critical theory. See also Margaret Alterton, *Origins of Poe's Critical Theory* (Iowa City: Univ. of Iowa Humanistic Studies, 1925) [PS2638/A5/1922]; Edmund Wilson, "Poe as a Literary Critic," *Nation*, 155 (31 October 1942), 452–53; and George Snell, "First of the New Critics," *Quarterly Review of Literature*, 2 (Summer 1945), 333–40. Poe's aesthetic is explained by Marvin Laser, "The Growth and Structure of Poe's Concept of Beauty," *Journal of English Literary History*, 15 (March 1948), 69–84 and again by

George Kelly, "Poe's Theory of Beauty," *American Literature,* 27 (January 1956), 521–36. Aspects of his fiction are doggedly reviewed by G. R. Thompson, *Poe's Fiction: Romantic Irony in the Gothic Tales* (Madison: Univ. of Wisconsin Press, 1973) [PS2638/T5].

Representative critical essays are collected in Eric W. Carlson, ed., *The Recognition of Edgar Allan Poe: Selected Criticism since 1829** (Ann Arbor: Univ. of Michigan Press, 1966) [PS2638/C34] and Robert Regan, ed., *Poe: A Collection of Critical Essays** (Englewood Cliffs, N.J.: Prentice-Hall, 1967) [PS2631/R38].

As the first volume of the *Collected Works of Edgar Allan Poe* projected by the Belknap Press of Harvard University Press, Thomas Ollive Mabbott's edition of the *Poems* (1969) [PN2600/F69] is the fruit of a lifetime of work and a model of textual scholarship that, in introduction and headnotes, establishes the provenance of every poem. Floyd Stovall, ed., *The Poems of Edgar Allan Poe* (Charlottesville: Univ. Press of Virginia, 1965) [PS2605/A1/1965a] is as attractive in format as it is instructive as an introduction to the poetry.

THE SCHOOLROOM POETS

The Schoolroom Poets, so called because for many years their venerable faces looked down from portraits on schoolroom walls, are William Cullen Bryant, John Greenleaf Whittier, Henry Wadsworth Longfellow, James Russell Lowell, and Oliver Wendell Holmes. These people were once thought to be among the most important writers of the nineteenth century. Changes in literary attitudes have now relegated them to lesser positions, but each of them in his own way was genuinely an artist, and none should be completely forgotten. George Arms, *The Fields Were Green: A New View of Bryant, Whittier, Holmes, Lowell, and Longfellow* (Stanford: Stanford Univ. Press, 1953) [PS541/A8] explains why they should be remembered and offers poems selected from their writings that may be thought worthy of continued life.

WILLIAM CULLEN BRYANT

For Bryant (1794–1878), the standard life remains that of his son-in-law, Parke Godwin, *A Biography of William Cullen Bryant, with Extracts from His Private Correspondence,* 2 vols. (New York:

Appleton, 1883) [PS1150/E83]. Briefer and probably more available are Harry Houston Peckham, *Gotham Yankee: A Biography of William Cullen Bryant* (New York: Vantage, 1950) [PS1181/P4] and Albert F. McLean, Jr., *William Cullen Bryant* (New York: Twayne, 1964) [PS1181/M3]. Even briefer, but excellent, is Van Wyck Brooks, "New York: Bryant," in Brooks's *The World of Washington Irving* (New York: Dutton, 1944) [PS208/B7].

JOHN GREENLEAF WHITTIER

For Whittier (1807–1892), the standard biography is Samuel T. Pickard, *Life and Letters of John Greenleaf Whittier*, 2 vols., rev. ed. (Boston and New York: Houghton Mifflin, 1907) [PS3281/P5/ 1894b]. More recent studies include Whitman Bennett, *Whittier: Bard of Freedom* (Chapel Hill: Univ. of North Carolina Press, 1941) [PS3281/B4]; John A. Pollard, *John Greenleaf Whittier, Friend of Man* (Boston: Houghton Mifflin, 1949) [PS3281/P6]; and Edward Wagenknecht, *John Greenleaf Whittier: A Portrait in Paradox* (New York: Oxford Univ. Press, 1967) [PS3281/W3]. Useful critical introductions are Lewis Leary, *John Greenleaf Whittier** (New York: Twayne, 1961) [PS3288/L4/1962]; John B. Pickard, *John Greenleaf Whittier: An Introduction and Interpretation** (New York: Barnes & Noble, 1961) [PS2381/P48]; and especially Robert Penn Warren, *John Greenleaf Whittier's Poetry: An Appraisal and a Selection,** (Minneapolis: Univ. of Minnesota Press, 1971) [PS3253/W3]. Pleasantly written to underscore the decencies of the poet as a man is Elizabeth Gray Vining, *Mr. Whittier: A Biography* (New York: Viking, 1974) [PS3281/V5].

HENRY WADSWORTH LONGFELLOW

By far the best study on Longfellow (1807–1882) is Newton Arvin, *Longfellow: His Life and Work* (Boston: Little, Brown, 1963) [PS2281/A6], but see also Lawrance Thompson, *Young Longfellow, 1807–1843* (New York: Macmillan, 1938) [PS2282/ T5], a masterly study of difficulties confronting a budding poet in early nineteenth-century America. Andrew Hilen, ed., *The Letters of Henry Wadsworth Longfellow*, 4 vols. (Cambridge: Belknap Press of Harvard Univ. Press, 1966–1972) [PS2281/A3H5] are revealing and often interesting. Lewis Leary, ed., *The Essential*

Longfellow (New York: Collier Books, 1963) [PS2252/L4] selects sixty poems "that reveal the poet at his best," but Howard Nemerov, ed., *Longfellow: Selected Poetry** (New York: Dell, 1959) [PS2252], as a selection of one poet's verse made by another poet, may reveal the better choice.

JAMES RUSSELL LOWELL

For Lowell (1819–1891), the most complete study is Martin B. Duberman, *James Russell Lowell* (Boston: Houghton Mifflin, 1966) [PS2331/D8]. Astute critical analysis is found in Leon Howard, *Victorian Knight Errant: A Study of the Early Literary Career of James Russell Lowell* (Berkeley: Univ. of California Press, 1952) [PS2331/H6]. Harry Hayden Clark and Norman Foerster, eds., *James Russell Lowell: Representative Selections* (New York: American Book Company, 1947) [PS2302/C5] contains a sound introduction and a useful bibliography.

OLIVER WENDELL HOLMES

The most informative study of the many-faceted career of Holmes (1809–1894) as physician, novelist, poet, and wit is Eleanor Marguerite Tilton, *Amiable Autocrat: A Biography of Oliver Wendell Holmes* (New York: Henry Schuman, 1947) [PS1981/T5]. M. A. De Wolfe Howe, *Holmes of the Breakfast Table* (New York: Oxford Univ. Press, 1936) [PS1981/H6] is an engaging appreciative account. Clarence P. Oberndorf, *The Psychiatric Novels of Oliver Wendell Holmes* (New York: Columbia Univ. Press, 1943) [PS1952/O2] contains recognitions by a modern physician of the insights of a predecessor. Samuel I. Hayakawa and Howard Mumford Jones, eds., *Oliver Wendell Holmes: Representative Selections* (New York: American Book Company, 1939) [PS1953/H4] contains a good introduction and bibliography.

WALLACE STEVENS (1879–1955)

Because Wallace Stevens is a complex poet, much of the writing that attempts to explain what he expressed, meant, or suggested is also complex. An introduction to what Stevens wrote and what until

1974 had been written about him is Joseph N. Riddel, "Wallace Stevens," in Jackson R. Bryer, ed., *Sixteen Modern American Authors: A Survey of Research and Criticism** (Durham, N.C.: Duke Univ. Press, 1974) [PS221/B7/1974]. J. M. Edelstein, *Wallace Stevens: A Descriptive Bibliography* (Pittsburgh: Univ. of Pittsburgh Press, 1973) [Z8842/7/E35] supersedes previous listings of writings by and about Stevens. The standard edition is *The Collected Poems of Wallace Stevens* (New York: Knopf, 1954) [PS3537/T4753/1954], to which, however, must be added *Opus Posthumous* (New York: Knopf, 1957) [PS3537/T4753A6/1957]. Adequate for an introduction is *Selected Poetry by Wallace Stevens*, ed. Samuel French Morse (New York: Vintage, 1959) [PS3537/T4753A6/1959]. A larger selection will be found in Holly Stevens, ed., *The Palm at the End of the Mind: Selected Poems and a Play** (New York: Knopf, 1971) [PS3537/T4753A6/1971], which corrects some errors in previous editions.

William Burney, *Wallace Stevens** (New York: Twayne, 1968) [PS3537/T4753Z6216] is a readable elementary introduction, though not always up-to-date on modern scholarship. Ronald Sukenick, *Wallace Stevens: Musing the Obscure. Readings and Interpretations, and a Guide to the Collected Poetry** (New York: New York Univ. Press, 1967) [PS3537/T4753Z768] is a useful guide to forty-seven of the most often discussed Stevens poems, but it must not be depended on for critical analysis in depth. Brief, but more sound, is Frank Kermode, *Wallace Stevens* (Edinburgh: Oliver and Boyd, 1960; New York: Grove, 1961) [PS3537/T4753Z67], which offers paraphrastical commentary on nearly all of Stevens's principal poems. William York Tindall, *Wallace Stevens* (Minneapolis: Univ. of Minnesota Press, 1961) [PS3537/T4753Z77] is a gracefully written brief survey that finds Stevens's talent rooted in a kind of symbolism inherited from abroad, especially from France.

The long-awaited critical biography by Stevens's literary executor, Samuel French Morse, *Wallace Stevens: Poetry As Life* (New York: Pegasus, 1970) [PS3537/T4753Z68], is to many critics a disappointingly unrevealing book. William Van O'Connor, *The Shaping Spirit: A Study of Wallace Stevens* (Chicago: Regnery, 1950) [PS3537/T4753Z7] reveals as much of the poet's life as was at that time known. Perhaps no detailed life can ever be written, for Stevens was a private man, public only in his activities as an insurance company executive in Hartford. His daughter has issued a generous selection of *Letters of Wallace Stevens*, ed. Holly Stevens (New York: Knopf, 1966) [PS3537/T4753/Z53], which contains portions of an early journal and headnotes that supply important biographical information. She also has in progress a complete commentary on the first half of her father's life, tentatively titled *Souvenirs and Prophecies*.

Of criticism there is plenty, sometimes as revealing of the predilections of the critic as of the poetry of the poet. Stevens himself says something of his intention in *The Necessary Angel: Essays on Reality and the Imagination*,* (New York: Knopf, 1951) [PN1055/ S8], but he says it in language which is often as elusive as that of his poetry. Recognition of his verbal precision and unique world view was early revealed by R. P. Blackmur, "Examples of Wallace Stevens," *Hound & Horn*, 5 (January-March 1932), 223–55. Other perceptive critical essays are Louis L. Martz, "Wallace Stevens: The Romance of the Precise," *Yale Poetry Review*, 2 (August 1946), 13–20, and his later influential "Wallace Stevens: The World as Meditation," *Yale Review*, 47 (Summer 1958), 517–76; Wylie Sypher, "Connoisseur in Chaos: Wallace Stevens," *Partisan Review*, 13 (Winter 1946), 83–94; and, especially perceptive, Marius Bewley, "The Poetry of Wallace Stevens," *Partisan Review*, 16 (September 1949), 895–915, and his later "The Poetry of Wallace Stevens," *Commonweal*, 62 (23 September 1955), 617–22. Poets speak well of Stevens's writings; see especially Randall Jarrell, "Reflections on Wallace Stevens," *Partisan Review*, 18 (May-June 1951), 335–42; Howard Nemerov, "The Poetry of Wallace Stevens," *Sewanee Review*, 65 (Winter 1957), 1–14; and John Crowe Ransom, "The Planetary Poet," *Kenyon Review*, 26 (Winter 1964), 233–64. Obscurity and decadence are discovered in his later verse by Yvor Winters, "Wallace Stevens, or the Hedonist's Progress," in Winters's *The Anatomy of Nonsense* (Norfolk, Conn.: New Directions, 1943) [PN99/U5W5]. Peter L. McNamara, "Wallace Stevens' Autumnal Doctrine," *Renascence*, 26 (Winter 1974), 73–85, effectively defends Stevens against this charge.

Roy Harvey Pearce, "Wallace Stevens: The Life of the Imagination," *PMLA*, 64 (September 1951), 561–82, is largely subsumed in his finely perceptive discussion in *The Continuity of American Poetry* (Princeton: Princeton Univ. Press, 1961) [PS303/P4], which places Stevens firmly within an American tradition. Of book-length critical studies, A. Walton Litz, *The Poetic Development of Wallace Stevens* (New York: Oxford Univ. Press, 1972) [PS3537/T4753/Z675] has been well received by other critics as a perceptive study of Stevens's progress as a poet; its major emphasis is on the early poems. Probably the most simply useful study is Joseph N. Riddel, *The Clairvoyant Eye: The Poetry and Poetics of Wallace Stevens** (Baton Rouge: Louisiana State Univ. Press, 1965) [PS3537/T4753/Z76], which examines both the poet's theory and practice. Daniel Fuchs, *The Comic Spirit of Wallace Stevens* (Durham, N.C.: Duke Univ. Press, 1963) [PS3537/T4753/Z64] is a valuable revelation of the cultural milieu in which Stevens wrote. Robert Buttel, *Wallace Stevens: The Making of "Harmonium"* (Princeton: Princeton Univ. Press, 1967) [PS3537/T4753/Z622] is an informative study of the poet's apprentice years. Frank Doggett, *Stevens' Poetry of Thought** (Baltimore: Johns Hopkins Press, 1966) [PS3537/T4753/Z625] relates the poet's development to the intellectual milieu of his time. James Baird, *The Dome and the Rock: Structure in the Poetry of Wallace Stevens* (Baltimore: Johns Hopkins Press, 1968) [PS3537/T4753] has important things to say about how Stevens made a poem. Helen Hennessy Vendler, *On Extended Wings: Wallace Stevens' Longer Poems* (Cambridge: Harvard Univ. Press, 1969) [PS3537/T4753/Z8/1969], through close descriptive explication, reveals progressive transformation in the poet's style.

Roy Harvey Pearce and J. Hillis Miller, eds., *The Act of the Mind: Essays on the Poetry of Wallace Stevens* (Baltimore: Johns Hopkins Press, 1965) [PS3537/T453/Z75] presents twelve critiques, the intention of which is "to take seriously Wallace Stevens's claims as a philosophical poet, and to study the implications, range, and import of those claims." Other useful gatherings are Ashley Brown and Robert S. Haller, eds., *The Achievement of Wallace Stevens* (Philadelphia: Lippincott, 1962) [PS3537/T4753/Z62]; Marie Borroff, ed., *Wallace Stevens: A Collection of Critical Essays** (Englewood Cliffs, N.J.: Prentice-Hall, 1963) [PS3537/T47/Z6]; and Peter L. McNamara, ed., *Critics on Wallace Stevens** (Coral Gables, Fla.: Univ. of Miami Press, 1973) [PS3537/T4753/Z678] 561–824, which contains eight essays subsumed under the general title "Wallace Stevens and the Romantic Heritage."

EDWARD TAYLOR (1645?–1729)

The poetry of Edward Taylor, virtually unknown until 1937, was first partially collected in Thomas H. Johnson, *The Poetical Works of Edward Taylor** (Princeton: Princeton Univ. Press, 1939) [PS850/T2], and Johnson added to the canon in "Topical Verses of Edward Taylor," *Publications of the Colonial Society of Massachusetts*, 34 (1943), 513–54, and "Some Edward Taylor Gleanings," *New England Quarterly*, 16 (June 1943), 280–96. An enlarged edition has been prepared, Donald E. Stanford, ed., *The Poems of Edward Taylor** (New Haven: Yale Univ. Press, 1960) [PS850/T2A6], an abridged paperback edition of which was issued in 1963. Donald E. Stanford, "Edward Taylor's Metrical History of Christianity," *American Literature*, 33 (November 1961), 279–95, presents an untitled long poem attributed to Taylor. No complete edition of the poems is yet available.

Norman S. Grabo, ed., *Edward Taylor's Christographia* (New Haven: Yale Univ. Press, 1962) [BX7117/T3] contains sermons delivered by Taylor during 1701–1703, each prefaced by a poetic meditation, and Grabo's edition of *Edward Taylor's Treatise Concerning the Lord's Supper* (East Lansing: Michigan State Univ. Press, 1966) [BX7239/L6T3/1966] presents eight sermons delivered in 1694. Francis Murphy, ed., *The Diary of Edward Taylor* (Springfield, Mass.: Connecticut Valley Historical Museum, 1964) [BX7260/T28A3] reveals few biographical facts. There is no biography, for biographical details are in large part presently unknown. The first full-length introduction to the man and his writings is Norman S. Grabo, *Edward Taylor** (New York: Twayne, 1961) [BX7260/T27G7/1962]; see also Donald E. Stanford, *Edward Taylor** (Minneapolis: Univ. of Minnesota Press, 1965) [PS850/T2Z8], which is brief but informative.

Taylor was first introduced by Thomas H. Johnson, "Edward Taylor: A Puritan 'Sacred Poet,'" *New England Quarterly*, 10 (June 1937), 290–322. Since then there have been varying, and sometimes conflicting, attempts to place Taylor in some literary or intellectual tradition. Among the better of these, their titles self-explanatory, are Austin Warren, "Edward Taylor's Poetry: Colonial Baroque," *Ken-*

yon Review, 3 (Summer 1941), 355–71; Wallace C. Brown, "Edward Taylor: American 'Metaphysical,'" *American Literature,* 16 (November 1944), 186–97; Nathalia Wright, "The Morality Tradition in the Poetry of Edward Taylor," *American Literature,* 18 (March 1946), 1–17; Willie T. Weathers, "Edward Taylor Hellenistic Puritan," *American Literature,* 18 (March 1946), 18–26; Roy Harvey Pearce, "Edward Taylor and the Cambridge Platonists," *American Literature,* 26 (March 1954), 1–33; and Norman S. Grabo, "Catholic Tradition, Puritan Literature and Edward Taylor," *Papers of the Michigan Academy of Science, Arts and Letters,* 45 (1960), 395–462. His place within a tradition is perhaps best set forth by Louis L. Martz in his introduction to Donald E. Stanford, ed., *The Poems of Edward Taylor,* cited above; see also Martz's *The Poetry of Meditation: A Study in English Religious Literature of the Seventeenth Century,** rev. ed. (New Haven: Yale Univ. Press, 1962) [PR549/R4M3/1962].

Other significant articles include William Manierre, II, "Verbal Patterns in the Poetry of Edward Taylor," *College English,* 23 (January 1962), 296–99; Evan Prosser, "Edward Taylor's Poetry," *New England Quarterly,* 40 (Summer 1967), 375–98; and Charles W. Mignon, "Edward Taylor's Preparatory Meditations: A Decorum of Imperfections," *PMLA,* 83 (December 1968), 1423–28. Also consult Constance J. Gefvert, *Edward Taylor: An Annotated Bibliography, 1668–1970* (Kent, Ohio: Kent State Univ. Press, 1971) [Z8861/4/G44].

HENRY DAVID THOREAU (1817–1862)

The Writings of Henry D. Thoreau, including his journals, are being published in twenty-five volumes by the Princeton University Press. Neither Walter Harding and Carl Bode, eds., *The Correspondence of Henry David Thoreau* (New York: New York Univ. Press, 1958) [PS3053/A3/1958], nor Carl Bode, ed., *The Collected Poems of Henry Thoreau,** enl. ed. (Baltimore: Johns Hopkins Press, 1964) [PS3041/B6/1964] is complete. William L. Howarth, *The Literary Manuscripts of Henry David Thoreau* (Columbus: Ohio State Univ. Press, 1974) [Z8873/H6] catalogues and locates everything that remains of what Thoreau ever wrote.

Walter Harding, *The Days of Henry Thoreau: A Biography*
(New York: Knopf, 1965) [PS3053/H3] is the most complete and
sympathetic account of Thoreau's life. It can be supplemented by
Ellery Channing, *Thoreau: The Poet Naturalist*, new ed. (Boston:
Goodspeed, 1902) [PS3053/C4/1902a], written by a man who knew
Thoreau and perhaps understood him better than any other, and by
Edward Waldo Emerson, *Henry Thoreau as Remembered by a
Young Friend* (Boston and New York: Houghton Mifflin, 1917)
[PS3053/E45]. Henry Seidel Canby, *Thoreau* (Boston: Houghton
Mifflin, 1939) [PS3053/C3] is an excellent narrative account except
when its author imagines that he finds Thoreau falling in love.
Milton Meltzer and Walter Harding, eds., *A Thoreau Profile** (New
York: Crowell, 1962) [PS3053/M4] is an attractive chronological
combination of illustrations and text.

Joseph Wood Krutch, *Henry David Thoreau** (New York: Sloane,
1948) [PS3053/K7] is a balanced introduction to the life and
writings. Reginald L. Cook, *Passage to Walden*, 2d ed. (New York:
Russell & Russell, 1966) [PS3057/N3C6/1966] presents a sound
appreciative interpretation. Ethel Seybold, *Thoreau, The Quest and
the Classics* (New Haven: Yale Univ. Press, 1951) [PS3057/
L55S4] is an important study of the origins and development of
Thoreau's ideas. John Aldrich Christie, *Thoreau as World Traveler*
(New York: Columbia Univ. Press, 1965) [PS3056/C4] explains
how a man who preferred to remain at home in Concord traveled
widely in his reading. James McIntosh, *Thoreau as Romantic
Naturalist: His Shifting Stance toward Nature* (Ithaca: Cornell
Univ. Press, 1974) [PS3057/N3M3] reads Thoreau against the
background of transatlantic romanticism; see also Perry Miller,
"Thoreau in the Context of International Romanticism," *New England
Quarterly*, 23 (June 1961), 147–59. Perry Miller, ed., *Consciousness at Concord: The Text of Thoreau's Hitherto "Lost
Journal," 1840–1841* (Boston: Houghton Mifflin, 1958) [PS3053/
A26] contains in its introduction a severe criticism of Thoreau as a
man and writer, as does Leon Edel, *Henry David Thoreau** (Minneapolis: Univ. of Minnesota Press, 1970) [PS3053/E4]. Walter
Harding, *A Thoreau Handbook** (New York: New York Univ.
Press, 1959) [PS3053/H32] gives a useful summary of Thoreau's
life, works, sources, ideas, and reputation.

A milestone in Thoreau scholarship is F. O. Matthiessen, "From

Emerson to Thoreau," *American Renaissance: Art and Expression in the Age of Emerson and Whitman** (New York: Oxford Univ. Press, 1941) [PS201/M3], which places Thoreau in a literary tradition that extended, not only to the past and to his New England contemporaries but also forward to important twentieth-century writers. He was ably seconded by Stanley E. Hyman, "Thoreau in Our Time," *Atlantic Monthly*, 178 (November 1946), 137–46, which finds Thoreau importantly in the "stream of American tradition." A second milestone is Sherman Paul, *The Shores of America: Thoreau's Inward Exploration** (Urbana: Univ. of Illinois Press, 1958) [PS3053/P3], which presents Thoreau as a literary aspirant assured of his destiny, laboring to maintain himself between appearances and truth, an artist who would "expand the principle of perception to structure: to create fables as well as symbols, or to make the structure itself symbolic." This view is substantiated in Laurence Stapleton, ed., *H. D. Thoreau: A Writer's Journal** (New York: Dover, 1960) [PS3053/A27], which brings together all Thoreau's statements of his ideals in craftsmanship, and in "Thoreau: The Concrete Vision," in her *The Elected Circle: Studies in the Art of Prose* (Princeton: Princeton Univ. Press, 1973) [PR751/S8], a sensitive and sensible examination of Thoreau's notion of what prose style might be.

A third milestone, not only in studies of Thoreau but in literary scholarship in general, is J. Lyndon Shanley, *The Making of Walden, with the Text of the First Version* (Chicago: Univ. of Chicago Press, 1957) [PS3048/S5], a book of painstaking detail and unassertive competence that demonstrates that textual study can be raised to the level of serviceable criticism as, through examination of successive versions of Walden from 1849 to 1854, Thoreau is revealed as a craftsman rounding out and filling in an intricately structured book. For further insight into that book, see Joseph J. Moldenhauer, "Images of Circularity in Thoreau's Prose," *Texas Studies in Literature and Language*, 1 (Summer 1959), 245–65, and his "The Extravagant Maneuver: Paradox in *Walden*," *Graduate Journal*, 6 (1964), 132–46. See also Walter Harding, "Five Ways of Looking at Walden," *Massachusetts Review*, 4 (Autumn 1962), 149–62. Charles R. Anderson, *The Magic Circle of Walden* (New York: Holt, Rinehart & Winston, 1968) [PS3048/A8] explores intricacies of structure and suggests that the book be read as if it were a poem. Further helpful commentary is brought together in Lauriat Lane, ed., *Approaches to Walden* (San Francisco: Wadsworth, 1961) [PS3048/L3] and Richard Ruland, ed., *Twentieth-Century Interpretations of Walden: A Collection of Critical Essays** (Englewood Cliffs, N.J.: Prentice-Hall, 1968) [PS3048/R8].

The influence of Thoreau's essay on "Resistance to Civil Government" is set forth in Walter Harding, ed., *The Variorum Civil Disobedience* (New York: Twayne, 1967) [JC328/T5/1967]. For its place in the intellectual context of its time, see Edward H. Madden, *Civil Disobedience and the Moral Law in Nineteenth-Century American Philosophy** (Seattle: Univ. of Washington Press, 1968) [B901/M3]. For reflections on its influence in our time, see Mark Harris, ed., *Days of Civil Disobedience: Henry David Thoreau's Essay on the Duty of Disobedience with Photographs of Recent Instances of Disobedience in the United States** (New York: War Resister's League, 1970), not usually available, however, in college libraries, and Ron McKuen, ed., *The Wind That Blows Is All That Anybody Knows: The Thoughts of Henry David Thoreau** (Los Angeles: Stanyan, 1970) [PS3042/M25]. Jerome Lawrence and Robert E. Lee, *The Night Thoreau Spent in Jail: A Play** (New York: Hill & Wang, 1970) [PS3523/A934/N5/1971] is an attractive, though not in every respect correct, revelation of Thoreau's view as a social reformer.

Much of the better criticism of Thoreau will be found in such volumes as Walter Harding, ed., *Thoreau: A Century of Criticism* (Dallas: Southern Methodist Univ. Press, 1954) [PS3054/H3]; Sherman Paul, ed., *Thoreau: A Collection of Critical Essays** (Englewood Cliffs, N.J.: Prentice-Hall, 1962) [PS3053/P33]; Walter Harding, ed., *The Thoreau Centennial: Papers Marking the Observance in New York City of the One Hundredth Anniversary of the Death of Henry David Thoreau* (Albany: State Univ. of New York Press, 1965) [PS3053/H315]; John H. Hicks, ed., *Thoreau in Our Season* (Amherst: Univ. of Massachusetts Press, 1966) [PS3053/H5], a reissue of "Thoreau: A Centenary Gathering," *Massachusetts Review*, 4 (Autumn 1962), 41–172; William Bysshe Stein, ed., *New Approaches to Thoreau: A Symposium* (Hartford, Conn.: Transcendental, 1969) [PS3054/N4]; and Wendell Glick, ed., *The Recognition of Henry David Thoreau: Selected Criticism Since 1848* (Ann Arbor: Univ. of Michigan Press, 1969) [PS3052/ G5/1969].

WALT WHITMAN (1819-1892)

The Collected Writings of Walt Whitman, including his correspondence and prose, is being issued in eighteen volumes by the New York University Press. Harold W. Blodgett and Sculley Bradley, eds., *Leaves of Grass: Comprehensive Reader's Edition* (New York: New York Univ. Press, 1965) [PS3201/1965] presents in one volume an accurate text of all Whitman's poems, together with a wide selection from surviving fragments; the same editors, together with William White, have announced a Variorum Edition of the poems, also to be published by the New York University Press. *Walt Whitman's Blue Book: The 1860-61 Leaves of Grass Containing His Manuscript Additions and Revisions,* 2 vols., the first volume a facsimile of the unique copy in the Oscar Lion Collection of the New York Public Library, and the second a textual analysis by Arthur Golden (New York: New York Public Library, 1968) [PS3201/1860c], is an invaluable revelation of Whitman's methods in revision and composition.

The standard work on the poet's life is Gay Wilson Allen, *The Solitary Singer: A Critical Biography of Walt Whitman,* rev. ed. (New York: New York Univ. Press, 1967) [PS3231/A69/1967], which traces "consecutively the physical life of the man, the growth of his mind, and the development of his art out of his physical and mental experiences." Also of importance are two European studies: Frederick Schyberg, *Walt Whitman* (New York: Columbia Univ. Press, 1951) [PS3231/S43] and the two volumes of Roger Asselineau, *The Evolution of Walt Whitman: The Creation of a Personality* (Cambridge: Belknap Press of Harvard Univ. Press, 1960) [PS3231/A833/v.1], and *The Evolution of Walt Whitman: The Creation of a Book* (Cambridge: Belknap Press of Harvard Univ. Press, 1960) [PS3231/A833/v.2]. Both Schyberg and Asselineau speculate on Whitman's sexual drives and their relationship to his approach to life and poetry. Henry Seidel Canby, *Walt Whitman: An American. A Study in Biography* (Boston: Houghton

Mifflin, 1943) [PS2331/C27] is a graceful introduction to the poet's "inner life and . . . the mysterious creative process of poetry." Van Wyck Brooks, *The Times of Melville and Whitman* (New York: Dutton, 1947) [PS201/B7] is more valuable for what it says of the times than of the poet. A reliable brief introduction to man and writings is Richard Chase, *Walt Whitman* (Minneapolis: Univ. of Minnesota Press, 1961) [PS3231/C45/1961].

All the books mentioned above contain valuable critical insights, but to them must be added George Santayana, "The Poetry of Barbarism," in his *Interpretations of Poetry and Religion* (New York: Scribner's, 1900) [PN1077/S2], which finds both Whitman and the English poet Robert Browning to be enemies of good taste in poetry. Also see the irreverent but perceptive insights in D. H. Lawrence, *Studies in Classic American Literature** (New York: Seltzer, 1923) [PS121/L3] and Randall Jarrell, "Walt Whitman: He Had His Nerve," *Kenyon Review*, 14 (Winter 1952), 63–79, reprinted in *Poetry and the Age** (New York: Knopf, 1953) [PN1271/J3], which scolds Whitman for pretending to be a deep thinker when he was, after all, nothing but a superb poet.

Newton Arvin, *Whitman* (New York: Macmillan, 1938) [PS3231/A8], as a product of its socially oriented times, interprets Whitman and his poetry in terms of the poet's social and political notions but contains valuable critical insights. Richard Chase, *Walt Whitman Reconsidered** (New York: Sloane, 1955) [PS3231/C47] is a freshly original view of Whitman, not only as "the supreme poet of American optimism and pragmatism, the rhapsodist of our material and spiritual forces," but also as a great and unmistakably native comic poet. Floyd Stovall, *The Foreground of Leaves of Grass* (Charlottesville: Univ. Press of Virginia, 1974) [PS3236/S8] evaluates aspects of Whitman's life that affected his intellectual development and influenced the direction of his poetry. James E. Miller, Jr., Karl Shapiro, and Bernice Slote, *Start with the Sun: Studies in Cosmic Poetry** (Lincoln: Univ. of Nebraska Press, 1960) [PS3238/M55] studies "the Whitman tradition" as it has grown and developed among later writers, as does Roy Harvey Pearce, *The Continuity of American Poetry* (Princeton: Princeton Univ. Press, 1961) [PS303/P4], which finds Whitman a source from which poets who have followed him have inevitably, though sometimes unconsciously, derived.

Especially useful as introductions are three books by James E. Miller, Jr.: *A Critical Guide to Leaves of Grass** (Chicago: Univ. of Chicago Press, 1957) [PS3238/M5], which contains structural analyses of individual poems and of the work as a whole; *Walt Whitman** (New York: Twayne, 1962) [PS3231/M5], which explicates in detail the better known poems; and *Whitman's "Song of Myself": Origin, Growth Meaning** (New York: Dodd, Mead, 1964) [PS3222/S6/1964]. Another useful explicatory guide, intended for classroom use, is Gay Wilson Allen and Charles T. Davis, *Walt Whitman's Poems: Selections with Critical Aids* (New York: New York Univ. Press, 1955) [PS3203/A5]. Howard J. Waskow, *Whitman: Explorations in Form* (Chicago: Univ. of Chicago Press, 1966) [PS3231/W35], concentrating on structure, sees the poems in relation to Whitman's thought and character, dividing them into four principal groups: the didactic, the imagistic, the narrative, and the subtly indirect. Edwin H. Miller, *Walt Whitman's Poetry: A Psychological Journey** (New York: New York Univ. Press, 1968) [PS3238/M45/1969], through lucid explanation of the poetry, shows underlying unities in image and theme. Gay Wilson Allen, *A Reader's Guide to Walt Whitman** (New York: Farrar, Straus and Giroux, 1970) [PS3231/A687] is a necessary desk book and bibliographical aid.

Collections of critical essays are numerous. Among the most useful are Milton Hindus, ed., *Leaves of Grass One Hundred Years After** (Stanford: Stanford Univ. Press, 1955) [PS3231/H5], which includes essays by William Carlos Williams, Leslie Fiedler, Richard Chase, Kenneth Burke, and others; R. W. B. Lewis, ed., *The Presence of Walt Whitman* (New York: Columbia Univ. Press, 1962) [PE1010/E5], which contains a particularly fine reading of "Out of the Cradle Endlessly Rocking" by Paul Fussell, Jr.; Roy Harvey Pearce, ed., *Whitman: A Collection of Critical Essays* (Englewood Cliffs, N.J.: Prentice-Hall, 1962) [PS3238/P4]; Edwin H. Miller, ed., *A Century of Whitman Criticism* (Bloomington: Indiana Univ. Press, 1969) [PS3238/M44/1969]; and Edwin H. Miller, ed., *The Artistic Legacy of Walt Whitman: A Tribute to Gay Wilson Allen* (New York: New York Univ. Press, 1970) [PS3238/A7].

CHAPTER ELEVEN
The Research Paper

ಞ ಞ ಞ A research paper is a formal, investigative essay with a thesis or an argument; that is, it explains or proves something. Its preparation therefore requires some pains, but need not be painful. If the subject is right, neither too large nor too small, and of interest to the writer, so that he pursues it with a creativity that moves beyond simple reliance on what other people have said, it can provide pleasure, both to the person who writes it and to the people who read it. Nothing is more time-wasting than to spend the hours and the energy necessary for the completion of a research paper on a subject that is of little interest to the writer, and which, therefore, will inevitably not attract responsive interest from a reader.

And who is the reader? Who is the research paper to be written for? The most obvious answer is that it is written to impress the person or persons who will grade it. But that may not be the correct answer. Ideally, a research paper should be written for one's peers, for people who have a general overall knowledge of the subject but do not know quite as much as the author has discovered about the specific matter on which the paper is written. Imagine that your paper is going to be read by the best informed of your classmates. Instructions given some years ago to contributors to the *Literary History of the United States* indicated that they were to think of their audience as the cultivated professional person—the lawyer, doctor, engineer, or teacher—who was interested in literature, knew some of it perhaps pretty well, but welcomed further information attractively but authoritatively presented. Most college instructors prefer that the student not direct his writing to them, but to a larger audience.

CHOOSING A SUBJECT

How to start? First, you will choose a subject or, perhaps to begin with, a general area that it would interest you to investigate. Then, you will determine what has previously been written about it, where, and by whom. In the preceding pages, information has been given on guides, bibliographies, histories of literature, and critical studies that in one way or another can be useful. For the ancient saying remains true, that education consists, not only in learning things, but also in learning where to find out about things. A student is known by the bibliographies he keeps—at first, in his head, things like lists of telephone numbers, addresses, and the names of textbooks that must be bought or borrowed, or books required for outside reading, until the list becomes too long or too complicated; then he must write it down. A bibliography is at first a shopping list, a convenient aid or jog to the memory. Finally, it becomes a record, a testimony about where in your investigatory journey you have been and a reminder of what you found there.

The longer you look, the more you will find. So you must begin to cut and prune extraneous, though often interesting, material in order to shape exactly what you want to say to a size that can fit attractively into the number of pages allowed you. Thus, you will begin to focus on some part of the general area that you have chosen. To write, for example, on the influence of Charles Dickens on nineteenth-century American fiction in ten pages, or even fifty, would be foolhardy, resulting only in a superficial overview. But to write on the influence of Dickens on character portrayal in selected, perhaps two, short stories by Bret Harte might prove to be interesting indeed. To write on the use of urban versus rural settings in American fiction would require a book-length manuscript. But to explain how Herman Melville in *Pierre* used country scenes and city scenes to intensify the meaning of that work might be very fruitful. To explain the world view that motivates the poetry of Wallace Stevens or Robert Frost would require much time and reading and could probably not be condensed to term-paper length. But to explicate a single poem, or a pair of poems, by either of these writers, or to suggest differences between them by comparing a poem, or a few poems, of each, could result in a short, but revealing paper.

Much has been written on American literature, but there is much more to write. To be a successful researcher, you will need to dig deeply within the territory on which you have staked temporary claim. You will know the place because of its relationship to other parts of the literary landscape that surround it, but you will not be distracted by nor disturb the attractive order of that landscape. More simply put, you will keep the subject within the bounds of what you can know or can discover.

Most important, you should write your paper on a subject that interests you. It will be a new thing because you have done it. For, though in writing your research paper, you will use facts and examples that have been pointed out before, what you write, if you write it well, will be unmistakably your own. Your attitudes, your background, your special knowledge of things and people, and the evidence that you have chosen to present as relevant—and that which you do not present because in your judgment it is irrelevant— all guarantee that what you say can be fresh and interesting, presenting a point of view that, when honestly set forth, must be seriously received.

GETTING STARTED

PREPARING A BIBLIOGRAPHY

As you begin to discover what other people have said on the topic you have chosen, start immediately to compile a working bibliography. For this purpose, most students use 4 x 6 cards on which to record potential sources, using one card for each source. Information on the card should include the author's name (last name first) exactly as it appears on the title page of the book or at the head (or end) of an essay or article. Then write the exact title of the book or essay, the place of publication, and the date of publication. If there are certain pages that you wish to remind yourself are of special importance, record them also. It is useful to record the library call number, usually in the upper lefthand corner of the card.

You will undoubtedly collect more references than you finally use. Those that do not prove helpful can be put aside. Those that remain will form the basis for your final bibliography.

Information for your preliminary or working bibliography can be found in at least four principal sources: (1) This volume can

PS
1888
F6   Fogle, Richard Harter. <u>Hawthorne's</u>

<u>Fiction: The Light and the Dark,</u>

rev. ed. Norman: Univ. of Oklahoma

Press, 1964.

(Especially pp. 138-67.)

```
Periodical
Room
        Holman, C. Hugh.   "Thomas Wolfe:

        A Bibliographical Study."   Texas

        Studies in Literature and Language

        1 (Spring 1958):   427-45.
```

provide a place to begin. The sources suggested herein will lead to further sources and larger bibliographies. Consult especially the rich store of information in the bibliographical volume of the *Literary History of the United States* [PS88/L522/1974]. (2) But so much new writing about American literature appears so regularly and so rapidly that even the surest guide is likely to be outdated by the time it appears. Consult, therefore, the annual MLA *International Bibliography* (1921–) [Z7006/M64] for data from more recent years and the quarterly listing of "Articles on American Literature Appearing in Current Periodicals," which appears in each issue of *American Literature*. Look through current periodicals that are likely to contain articles relating to your subject. Constant exploration, quick ingeniousness, and eternal vigilance are hallmarks of the successful researcher. (3) The card catalogue of your library is a fruitful further source of information. Most catalogues are arranged alphabetically according to author, title, and subject. The call number for each book is usually found in the upper lefthand corner of the card (just as it is on your bibliographical cards). This indicates where the book you seek is located in the library. Watch especially for bibliographies: there is hardly a writer or a subject in

American literature on which some industrious person has not compiled a bibliography. (4) Finally, you will discover that one reference
leads to another. Almost every book, article, or bibliography that
you consult will contain footnotes and/or bibliographies which will
lead you to other sources.

But do not overlook human potentials. Researchers are likely to
cluster together, for a coffee, coke, or cigarette break, and they are
often compulsive swappers of information. Furthermore, every researcher quickly learns that among the most generously helpful
people on his campus are members of the library staff, who are de-
lighted to help run down some obscure reference or suggest some
new source of information that the researcher has overlooked. But,
one caution! Look first. Few things are more embarrassing than to
have a librarian lead you to a card catalogue or some other easily
available reference source which, if you had been even a bit enterprising, you would have found for yourself.

Even professors can often be helpful. They are often flattered to
discover that you are investigating a subject in which they have
been especially interested. Learning to know professors, and learning
who among them can be approached and on what subject, is probably a pretty important part of an overall college education. Talk
also with your classmates—or with other students who just may have
been reading something that can be helpful to you. Graduate
students, when available, can be particularly helpful, and they are
usually happy to share what they have so recently learned. Scholarship, when it is at its best, is a cooperative enterprise, one person
feeding another to the ultimate well-being of all. This, however, is
not to suggest that what you write will not be yours. In courtesy, you
will acknowledge whatever help has been given, but what you have
to say and how you say it is a responsibility that is yours alone.

Perhaps courtesy is a thing to keep most firmly in mind in preparing a research paper. Writing clearly and interestingly is a courtesy
to every reader. Footnotes are both courteous acknowledgments of
assistance and indications to readers of the authority on which you
make statements or from whom some particularly apt quotation is
taken and where it can be found in larger context. A bibliography is
a courteous advisement of where further information on the subject
on which you have written may be found. If your handwriting is not

particularly legible, typing the research paper is certainly a courtesy to the person or persons who must read it.

TAKING NOTES

Many students take too many notes, and many take too few. Experience usually brings about a proper balance, but experience also suggests better too many than too few. Extraneous materials can always be discarded. Information not recorded but later discovered to be necessary means a time-consuming retracing of steps, extra trips to the library, or new searches through a book or an article for something that you are sure you remember to have seen somewhere but cannot remember where.

Notes are usually taken on 4 x 6 cards, with one piece of information recorded on each card. Using a notebook may seem easier at first, but is finally found to be inefficient because the notes cannot easily be filed in proper order. Using separate sheets of paper is also inefficient—and wasteful: the temptation often is to record too much in order to fill the page. On the 4 x 6 card, indicate the author from whom you quote, paraphrase, or summarize, and indicate by short title the book or the article: you already have completed a bibliographical card that gives complete information about the source. Then supply a word or phrase that identifies the subject or topic of the note and the page or pages on which the information is found. If you quote, be sure to use quotation marks; if you paraphrase or summarize, do not. This is very important, for it is easy to forget to place the quotation marks and then, when using the information, to forget that they should have been there, and thus, without meaning to at all, open yourself to charges of plagiarism.

On the following two pages are examples of note cards recording quotation, paraphrase, and finally, summary.

Quotation

```
Fogle, Hawthorne's Fiction          p. 57

            No simple meanings

"The significance of 'Ethan Brand' does not

lie, then, simply in the praise of the normal,

for in this instance the normal is not always

attractive.  The story will not bear the bur-

den of a simple meaning."
```

Paraphrase

```
Fogle, Hawthorne's Fiction          p. 57

            No simple meanings

There is more to the story of "Ethan Brand"

than a celebration of normality; there is no

simple meaning in this tale.
```

Summary

```
    Fogle, Hawthorne's Fiction        pp. 50-57

              No simple meanings

    There are no simple meanings in Hawthorne's

    fiction.  In "Ethan Brand," which seems to be

    an allegory, everything seems to suggest

    meanings:  the shadows, the sunlight, the

    fire, the cavernous kiln, and the people who

    cluster around it, but to find a single or a

    simple meaning is impossible.
```

MAKING AN OUTLINE

An outline is necessary, either in your head or on paper. The outline is a road map that keeps you on course. It is a practical tool that guarantees a logical, consecutive presentation of what you intend to demonstrate. It is an important semifinal overview of what you have found to say—and of how and in what order you will say it. It provides a skeletal outline for your paper. If what you have collected in notecards and bibliography cannot be fitted into an outline that is logical and coherent, then something has gone wrong. Perhaps you have missed material that is necessary for your demonstration. Perhaps some of the notes you have gathered are irrelevant. There is no surer way of finding out than by arranging the notes into a logical progression, an outline.

Some prefer to make a topic outline; others discover that their thinking is immensely assisted when they write each element of the outline as a complete sentence. But whichever form is used, the outline should contain, first, a statement of thesis—what the research paper sets out to prove—followed by concise statements, listed in logical order, of arguments that you will use to prove that thesis, and finally a conclusion in which your argument or demonstration is firmly clinched. It might take the following form:

Thesis statement:
Introduction
  I.
    A.
    B.
      1.
      2.
      3.
  II.
    A.
      1.
      2.
    B.
    C.
  III.
    A.
      1.
      2.
    B.
Conclusion:

What such an outline suggests is that there are three main ideas (represented by the numerals I, II, III), each of which is supported by secondary ideas or subcategories. There must be a logical reason why, for example, point III follows naturally from the last subcategory under point II, or that the Conclusion is a logical extension of the second main category under point III. You may discover that you have, not three points, but four or five. If you go beyond that number, you probably have too much material for a research paper of a length usually prescribed.

WRITING THE PAPER

No one can tell you how finally to write a research paper. Be simple and direct. Avoid professional clichés. Try to resist being condescending to your reader by using such hackneyed expressions as "of course" and "as everybody knows." Speak in your own voice rather than that of your sources: a research paper is not a string of quotations from other people casually strung together; it is, someone has said, an amalgam of your ideas and of selected documentation that supports what you have to say. After all, it is your paper, and only you can write it. So, good luck.

There are, however, a few formalities, matters of courtesy, that should be followed.

1. In writing the titles of books, articles, stories, poems, and your own research paper, capitalize all words except conjunctions, articles, and prepositions. Some find it helpful to remember that the first letter of each of the kinds of words *not* to be capitalized, when put together, spells "cap."

2. Short prose quotations are to be run into the text and enclosed in double quotation marks.

As Henry David Thoreau observed, "The mass of men lead lives of quiet desperation."

3. A quotation of more than four typewritten lines, or of more than one sentence, is to be set off from the text by three spaces and indented in block form five spaces from the left margin; it is usually single-spaced (though some instructions or instructors prefer it to be double-spaced) with no quotation marks at the beginning or end.

The first chapter of *Walden* contains a statement by Thoreau that many people think to be representative of his total philosophy:

> The mass of men lead lives of quiet desperation. What is called resignation is confirmed desperation. From the desperate city you go to the desperate country, and have to console yourself with the bravery of minks and muskrats. A stereotyped but unconscious despair is concealed even under what are called the games and amusements of mankind.

The first line of the above quotation is indented because, in *Walden*, the material quoted occurs at the beginning of a paragraph; if the material quoted comes from the middle of a paragraph, the first line is not indented.

4. When part of a quotation is omitted, the omission is indicated by three spaced periods.

The first chapter of *Walden* contains a statement by Thoreau that many people think to be representative of his total thought:

> The mass of men lead lives of quiet desperation. . . . A stereotyped but unconscious despair is concealed under what are called the games and amusements of mankind.

or

As Thoreau once said, most men "lead lives of . . . desperation."

5. When something is added to a quotation in order to clarify it, the addition is enclosed in square brackets.

As Henry Thoreau of Concord once observed, "The mass of men [of his time and place] lead lives of quiet desperation."

6. Poetry of more than two lines in length is set off from the text and centered on the page, usually typed with double spacing, with no quotation marks at the beginning or end.

Walt Whitman begins his "Song of Myself" with a bold assertion:

> I celebrate myself, and sing myself
> And what I assume you shall assume,
> For every atom belonging to me as good
>   belongs to you.

7. Poetry of two lines may be run into the text, enclosed in double quotation marks, and the division between lines indicated by a diagonal line:

Walt Whitman begins his "Song of Myself" with a bold assertion, "I celebrate myself, and sing myself, / And what I assume you shall assume."

DOCUMENTATION

It cannot be emphasized too often that the formalities of scholarship, whether in the use of quotations within a text or in footnoting and preparing bibliographies, are matters of courtesy. They are regularized procedures that make it possible for a reader easily to recognize exactly what the writer is doing and on what authority he does it. The forms suggested below correspond to those outlined in more detail in the manual issued by the Modern Language Association of America, *The MLA Style Sheet,* second edition, 1970 [Z253/ M73/1970]. But the forms suggested are not the only forms ever used. Other manuals and guides suggest forms that are in some details different. *The MLA Style Sheet,* however, is increasingly becoming the standard authority, recognized by most scholarly journals and publishing houses. Unless something else is recommended to them by their instructors, students will find it a trustworthy, competent guide. If it is not available in your college bookstore or library, a copy may be obtained from the Materials Center, Modern Language Association of America, 62 Fifth Avenue, New York, N.Y. 10011.

FOOTNOTES

The use of footnotes is a special form of politeness. To use too few is to deny a reader opportunity to follow up and investigate further something you have said or suggested. To use too many is to be pretentious or confusing, even insulting. Footnotes are acknowledgments of debts. They are also courteous guides. But they can become addictive. Someone has said that, like fine wines, footnotes should be used whenever beneficial, but not too much or too often.

A footnote may fulfill either of two general functions: (1) most often it cites the source of a direct quotation or the paraphrasing or summarizing of what someone else has said; (2) a footnote may be used to give information or present arguments that are germane to what is said in the body of the text but that, if included there, would be distracting or tangential.

Footnotes should be numbered consecutively throughout the research paper, beginning with 1. The numbers in the text that refer to footnotes appear at the end of the statement or quotation they identify and are raised slightly above the line, like this [1]. Do not use asterisks or other symbols. In a research paper, footnotes usually do not appear at the foot of the page on which the reference that they identify appears; rather, they appear consecutively at the end of the paper on a new page, double-spaced, with the first line of the footnote indented and the identifying number raised slightly. Check with your instructor on this matter, however.

FIRST FOOTNOTE REFERENCES TO BOOKS OR PARTS OF BOOKS

The following information is necessary in every first reference to a book or part of a book in a footnote: (1) the author or authors' names in normal order, followed by a comma; (2) the title of the book underlined (if an essay or a chapter in a book is cited, the title of the essay or chapter is enclosed in quotation marks, with a comma preceding the closing quotation mark, followed by the underlined title of the book in which the essay or chapter appears); (3) within parentheses, the place of publication followed by a colon, the name of the publisher, followed by a comma, the date of publication, the closing parenthesis followed by a comma; (4) the page reference in arabic numeral(s), preceded by the initial p. for page or pp. for pages [example: p. 116; pp. 116–18], followed by a period. If the work cited is in two or more volumes, the volume number is indicated with a roman numeral, placed before the page number, and followed by a comma and an indication of the page or pages *without* the abbreviation p. or pp. [example: II, 89–92]. When the reference is to a footnote on the page cited, the indication would be p. 4, n. 3, or II, 4, n. 3.

SUGGESTIONS AND PRECAUTIONS

(1) always take the title of a book from its title page, not from its cover or dust jacket; (2) in designating the place of publication, include the name of the state if the city in which the book was published is not readily identifiable; cite, for example (Boston: Houghton Mifflin, 1975), but (Norfolk, Conn.: New Directions, 1975); but do not cite the state, even when the city is not easily identified, if the name of the publisher includes the name of the state—(Lincoln: Univ. of Nebraska Press, 1975), but (Durham, N.C.: Duke Univ. Press, 1975). Note that the word "University" may be, but need not be, abbreviated; (3) the names of well-known publishers may be listed in shortened form: "Scribner's" instead of "Charles Scribner's Sons" or "Macmillan" instead of "The Macmillan Company." And the words "Company," "Publisher," or "Publishers" are often omitted or abbreviated—but when in doubt as to what may or may not be omitted or abbreviated, cite the name of the publisher exactly as it appears on the title page, for it is never incorrect to be complete; (4)

the date of publication of a book normally used to be found on the title page following the name of the publisher, but in recent books it is found on the back (the verso) of the title page.

The examples that follow will suggest footnote forms used to identify quotations or references to books of several kinds:

1. A book by a single author:

   [1] F. O. Matthiessen, *American Renaissance: Art and Expression in the Age of Emerson and Whitman* (New York: Oxford Univ. Press, 1940), pp. 128–29.

   (The subtitle, *Art and Expression in the Age of Emerson and Whitman*, may be omitted in a footnote reference. It must, however, appear when the book is listed in the bibliography.)

   [2] Randall Jarrell, "Reflections on Wallace Stevens," *Poetry and the Age* (New York: Knopf, 1953), p. 129.

   If, however, the author's name has been mentioned in the text, it is not necessary to repeat it in the footnote.

   [3] "Reflections on Wallace Stevens," *Poetry and the Age* (New York: Knopf, 1953), p. 129.

   If both the author's name and the title of the essay are mentioned in the text, both may be omitted in the footnote.

   [4] *Poetry and the Age* (New York: Knopf, 1953), p. 129.

2. A book by two or more authors:

   [5] Blyden Jackson and Louis D. Rubin, Jr., *Black Poetry in America* (Baton Rouge: Louisiana State Univ. Press, 1974), p. 42.

   [6] Frederick J. Hoffman, Charles Allen, and Carolyn F. Ulrich, *The Little Magazine: A History and a Bibliography* (Princeton: Princeton Univ. Press, 1945), pp. 192–204.

   When there are more than three authors, the customary practice is to list the citation as follows:

   [7] Robert E. Spiller et al., *Literary History of the United States* (New York: Macmillan, 1949), pp. xvii–xxii.

3. A work in two or more volumes:

   [8] Stanley T. Williams, *The Spanish Background of American*

Literature (New Haven: Yale Univ. Press, 1955), I, 346.

Note that, following the volume reference in roman numerals (I, II, III, IV, etc.), the initial "p" preceding the page reference is omitted.

[9] George C. D. Odell, *Annals of the New York Stage*, I (New York: Columbia Univ. Press, 1927), 578.

The volume citation placed before the parenthesis, as above, indicates that the several volumes that make up the work were not all published in the same year, but that volume I, cited, appeared in 1927.

4. An editor:

[10] Norman Holmes Pearson, ed., *The Complete Novels and Selected Tales of Nathaniel Hawthorne* (New York: Random House, 1937), p. 257.

5. An essay within a collection:

[11] William Harmon, "'Anti-Fiction' in American Humor," in *The Comic Imagination in America*, ed. Louis D. Rubin, Jr. (New Brunswick, N.J.: Rutgers Univ. Press, 1973), pp. 398–401.

6. A new edition:

[12] Babette Deutsch, *Poetry Handbook*, 4th ed. (New York: Funk & Wagnalls, 1974), pp. 16–19.

A new edition is one that has been revised or expanded.

7. A modern reprint of an old edition:

[13] George C. D. Odell, *Annals of the New York Stage* (1927; rpt. New York: AMS Press, 1970), I, 221.

8. An anonymous work:

[14] *Who Was Who in America*, I (Chicago: Marquis, 1943), 1262.

9. An unpublished dissertation or thesis:

[15] Elsie W. West, "The Gentle Flute: Washington Irving as Biographer," unpubl. diss. (Columbia Univ., 1965), p. 247.

10. A manuscript volume:

[16] Notebook 23, p. 50, Mark Twain Papers, Univ. of California, Berkeley.

[17] Notebook 23, TS, p. 50, Mark Twain Papers, Univ. of California, Berkeley.

The "TS" preceding the page reference above indicates that a typescript copy of the manuscript notebook had been used.

FOOTNOTE REFERENCES TO ARTICLES IN PERIODICALS

For footnotes referring to most articles in periodicals, the following information is necessary: (1) the author's name in normal order, followed by a comma; (2) the complete title of the article followed by a comma, all enclosed in quotation marks; (3) the name of the periodical underlined, followed by a comma; (4) the volume number in arabic numerals (for exceptions to this, see recommendations 6 and 8 below); (5) the date of publication of the periodical within parentheses, a comma following the closing parenthesis (for exceptions, see recommendations 6 and 8 below); and (6) the page or pages from which the material cited is quoted or, if the whole article is cited or recommended, the complete pagination of the article.

The following recommendations may help to clarify the above instructions:

1. An article from a journal with continuous pagination throughout an annual volume; most of the periodicals normally used by a student of American literature fall within this category.

    [2] R. P. Blackmur, "The Loose and Baggy Monsters of Henry James," *Accent*, 11 (1951), 132–33.

    The above form is authorized by *The MLA Style Sheet*. Some students, however, prefer to give complete documentation, principally as a courtesy to the reader; therefore, the following form has been used throughout the body of the text of this research guide:

    [2] R. P. Blackmur, "The Loose and Baggy Monsters of Henry James," *Accent*, 11 (Summer 1951), 132–33.

2. An article in a journal that pages each issue separately:

[3] John R. Frey, "America and Her Literature Reviewed by Postwar Germany," *American-Germanic Review*, 20 (June–July 1954), 31.

3. An article from a periodical that does not number volumes, but numbers issues only:

[4] Richard Hibler, "Thoreau and Epicurus," *Thoreau Society Bulletin*, No. 129 (February 1974), 2–3.

4. An article from a monthly magazine:

[5] Thornton Wilder, "Toward an American Language," *Atlantic Monthly*, July 1952, pp. 34–36.

The above form is authorized by *The MLA Style Sheet*; some, however, prefer to give complete documentation:

[6] Thornton Wilder, "Toward an American Language," *Atlantic Monthly*, 180 (July 1952), 34–36.

5. An article from a weekly periodical:

[7] Henry Steele Commager, "Noah Webster, 1758–1958: Schoolmaster to America," *Saturday Review*, 18 October 1958, pp. 3–4.

The above form is authorized by *The MLA Style Sheet*; some, however, prefer to give complete documentation:

[8] Henry Steele Commager, "Noah Webster, 1758–1958: Schoolmaster to America," *Saturday Review*, 41 (18 October 1958), 3–4.

6. An anonymous article:

[9] "Sinclair Lewis Dies in Italy," *Life,* 22 January 1951, p. 69.
or

[10] "Sinclair Lewis Dies in Italy," *Life,* 30 (22 January 1951), 69.

7. An item from a newspaper:

[11] "Funeral for Edwin Arlington Robinson," *New York Herald Tribune,* 7 April 1935, p. 17.

When the name of the city in which the newspaper is published is part of the title of the newspaper, it is underlined; when the name of the city is not part of the title of the newspaper, it is included in the footnote citation for the purpose of identification, but it is not underlined:

[12] "Dog Eat Dog," Raleigh *News and Observer*, 15 March 1974, p. 12.

When the newspaper is divided into sections, each of which is numbered separately, or when it appears in several editions, all of which may not contain exactly the same material or the same material in the same place, be sure to be courteously specific:

[13] "Ezra in Turmoil," *New York Times*, Late city ed., 7 January 1970, Sec. 6, p. 14.

SUBSEQUENT REFERENCES TO THE SAME BOOK OR ARTICLE

A full citation is not needed for footnote references to a book or article that has already been cited in a footnote. A shortened but intelligible form is used. For example, when you have cited:

[1] Arthur Hobson Quinn, *Edgar Allan Poe: A Critical Biography* (New York: Appleton-Century, 1941), p. 14.

further references to that volume may be shortened to:

[2] Quinn, *Poe*, p. 67.

Or, having cited:

[3] M. Thomas Inge, "Faulkner, the Man and His Masks: A Biographical Note," *Southern Observer*, 11 (March 1964), 55.

further reference to that article may be shortened to:

[4] Inge, "Faulkner, the Man and His Masks," p. 57.

If two or more footnotes in succession refer to the same source, it is sufficient to repeat the author's name and cite the page number:

[5] Inge, p. 58.

In a case like the above, it is also possible to use the Latin abbreviation "Ibid." (deriving from ibidem, the same):

[6] Ibid., p. 56

If the page reference, however, is the same as in the note immediately preceding, no page number is needed:

[7] Ibid.

But the use of "ibid" and other Latin words or abbreviations once commonly in use, such as "op. cit." (an abbreviation for *opus citatum,* the work cited), "loc. cit." (an abbreviation for *locus citatum,* the place cited), "supra" for above, and "infra" for below, is no longer recommended.

THE FINAL BIBLIOGRAPHY

A full bibliography of all sources used in the writing of the research paper is prepared on separate sheets and placed at the end of the paper, following the pages that contain footnote references. It is usually headed "A Selected Bibliography" or "List of Works Consulted." Included in it are only those works actually used in the writing of the research paper. Do not include all the works that you noted in your preliminary bibliography.

The form for a bibliographical entry differs from that of a footnote entry in three principal respects: (1) the author's name is written in reverse order, the last name first (when a work has two or more authors, only the name of the first is written in reverse order); (2) each of the three main divisions of the citation—the name of the author, the title of the work, and information on where and when the work was published—is followed by a period; and (3) the second line of the bibliographical entry is indented.

The following sample bibliography illustrates several of the forms that items in a bibliography may take:

Blackmur, R. P. "The Loose and Baggy Monsters of Henry James." *Accent,* 11 (Summer 1951), 129–36.

Jackson, Blyden, and Louis D. Rubin, Jr. *Black Poetry in America: Two Essays in Historical Interpretation.* Baton Rouge: Louisiana State Univ. Press, 1974.

Jarrell, Randall. "Reflections on Wallace Stevens." *Poetry and the Age.* New York: Knopf, 1953. Pages 121–34.

Notebook 23. Mark Twain Papers, Univ. of California, Berkeley.

When no author is given, an item in a bibliography enters the alphabetical order according to the first letter of its title. The next item, however, might have been entered—following Blackmur, R. P., above—as:

[Clemens, Samuel L.] Notebook 23. Mark Twain Papers, Univ. of California, Berkeley.

The name enclosed in square brackets indicates information that is not contained in the bibliographical item cited but that is supplied by the writer of the research paper.

West, Elsie B. "The Gentle Flute: Washington Irving as Biographer." Unpubl. diss. Columbia, 1965.

Williams, Stanley T. *The Spanish Backgrounds of American Literature*. 2 vols. New Haven: Yale Univ. Press, 1955.

A SAMPLE PAPER

The following pages contain a sample research paper, illustrating some of the points that have been discussed in this chapter.

F. Scott Fitzgerald's Women:

The Real Romantics

John Francis
English 83
27 April 1975

All the romantic young men in F. Scott Fitzgerald's novels fare badly. Amory Blaine in This Side of Paradise winds up something like a bum; Anthony Patch in The Beautiful and Damned gets pushed around in a wheelchair; the great Gatsby is brutally disillusioned and then shot; and in Tender Is the Night, Dick Diver drifts off among nameless towns of New York's Finger Lakes district. The women in the books manage to survive, however, and our temptation is to dismiss them as heartless, enterprising realists. Certainly they lack virtues--for one, nine-tenths of loyalty is unknown to them. Nonetheless, they are never condemned by the fallen heroes; Gatsby and Dick Diver, in fact, wish them the very best right to the end. For all their hardness and selfishness, the women in Fitzgerald's novels have redeeming characteristics; they actually seem closer to a genuine romanticism, as Fitzgerald himself finally understood and admired it, than the men are.

Fortunately, one of Fitzgerald's heroes actually discusses the issue of romanticism. Rosalind asks Amory Blaine, "You're not sentimental?" He counters, "No, I'm a romantic-- a sentimental person thinks things will last-- a romantic person hopes against hope that they won't."[1] Later in the book Amory will repeat this neat formulation to Eleanor. "I'm not sentimental--I'm as romantic as you are. The idea, you know, is that the sentimental person thinks things will last--the romantic person has a desperate confidence that they won't." Eleanor answers, "Epigrams. I'm going home" (p.229). She's right. Most of the men think they're romantic, as romantic as the women, and they think they have left the past behind, but they haven't. Even this first novel ends with Amory, a failure, walking the paths of his college days at Princeton, clinging to vanished dreams and saddled with "the pain of memory;

the regret for his lost youth" (p. 282). Any
poignancy he feels is really sentiment, a
backward-looking sadness, a degenerating melancholy.

But the women are different. Their
present is not made poignant by their past, but
by their _future_. Rosalind tells Amory, "Beauty
and love pass, I know. . . . Oh, there's sadness, too. I suppose all great happiness is a
little sad. Beauty means the scent of roses
and then the death of roses--" (_This Side of
Paradise_, p. 188). This is an essential theme
of F. Scott Fitzgerald's favorite poet, John
Keats.[2] In the "Ode to Melancholy" Keats
urges,

> Then glut thy sorrow on a morning
>   rose,
> . . . .
> Or if thy mistress some rich anger
>   shows,
> Emprison her soft hand, and let her
>   rave,
> And feed deep, deep upon her peerless
>   eyes.
> She dwells with Beauty--Beauty that
>   must die.[3]

Fitzgerald's women heighten their happiness with an awareness that the present is precious, a sadly momentary joy that soon must pass away.

Fitzgerald's men not only dwell on the past; they think they can bring it back, or at least freeze the present. We remember Gatsby's startling response to Nick Carraway, "'Can't repeat the past?' he cried incredulously. Why of course you can!"[4] But the women know much better what can and what cannot be done, and they are almost merciless in their knowledge. In The Beautiful and Damned, when Gloria and Anthony visit Lee's home at Arlington, Gloria is appalled and feels it is all a sacrilege:

> "I think it's perfectly terrible!"
> she said furiously, "the idea of letting
> these people come here! And of encour-
> aging them by making these houses show-
> places."
> "Well," objected Anthony, "if they
> weren't kept up they'd go to pieces."
> "What if they did!" she exclaimed
> as they sought the wide pillared porch.
> "Do you think they've left a breath of
> 1860 here? This has become a thing of
> 1914."
> "Don't you want to preserve old

things?"

"But you <u>can't</u>, Anthony. Beautiful things grow to a certain height and then they fade off, breathing out memories as they decay. . . ."

"Would you value your Keats letter if the signature was traced over to make it last longer? . . . There's no beauty without poignancy and there's no poignancy without the feeling that it's going, men, names, books, houses--bound for dust-- mortal--"[5]

Gloria combines an admittedly rare sensitivity to beauty with a natural acceptance of its inevitable decay, and her viewpoint seems a virtue. Her mercilessness and her hardness are finally even attractive.[6] The women in the other Fitzgerald novels participate to a lesser extent in her type, and in them the mercilessness is less romantic. Daisy can turn from Gatsby, Nicole from Dick, Rosalind from Amory-- all because they can harden themselves to the deterioration of the past. They will never be the scorned sentimentalists that Amory Blaine defines. While the Glorias look toward the changing future and grow sweetly melancholy,

the sentimental men dwell on the receding past
and grow desperate.

For all their hardness, Fitzgerald's women
share a wonderful sense of mystery. Nicole, in
Tender Is the Night, is a bizarre, charming
woman when Dick meets her at the sanitorium,
and even Rosemary Hoyt admires her elusiveness.
Daisy Buchanan, for Gatsby, is a mysterious
essence of wealth, and in her voice is an un-
canny vibrancy. Gloria Gilbert, in The Beautiful and Damned, is almost a mythic figure,
first described as "Beauty, who was born anew
every hundred years" (p. 27). All this mystery
proves specious, however, as one by one, the
women reveal that they have their feet planted
firmly on the ground. Nicole even admits it as
she prepares for her new soldier-of-fortune
lover, Tommy Barban: "How good to have things
like this, to be worshipped again, to pretend
to have a mystery!"[7] Yet in spite of this
cynicism she retains a romantic allure, as well

as the romantic habit: "She looked micro-
scopically at the lines of her flanks,
wondering how soon the fine, slim edifice would
begin to sink squat and earthward. In about
six years, but now I'll do--in fact, I'll do as
well as any one I know" (Tender Is the Night,
p. 290). At twenty-nine she does not think of
the past and grow sad; she thinks of the inevitable future and grows exhilarated with the
present. Dick, however, at this point is
feebly pursuing a much younger woman who,
according to Sergio Perosa, "has become his
only hope for rebirth and liberation";[8] he is
also failing pitifully at attempts to impress
newcomers with his college-days acrobatics.

In The Great Gatsby we see that the
falsely romantic hero has failed, but somehow
we can't entirely forsake his vision. Fitzgerald still seems partly charmed when he lets
Nick Carraway describe Gatsby's last moments.
It is an extraordinarily enraptured way of

describing emptiness.

> No telephone message arrived, but
> the butler went without his sleep and
> waited for it until four o'clock--until
> long after there was any one to give it
> to if it came. I have an idea that Gatsby
> himself didn't believe it would come, and
> perhaps he no longer cared. If that was
> true he must have felt that he had lost
> the old warm world, paid a high price for
> living too long with a single dream. He
> must have looked up at an unfamiliar sky
> through frightening leaves and shivered
> as he found what a grotesque thing a rose
> is and how raw the sunlight was upon the
> scarcely created grass. A new world,
> material without being real. . . . (p.142)

And the glorious last page, so full of pessim-

ism, is nonetheless inspired poetry. We almost

miss the gloom of the theme in the magnificent

rhythms and metaphors. Gatsby somehow still

seems right, at least in tone, and Daisy ab-

solutely wrong. Yet in Tender Is the Night,

written eight years later, Fitzgerald has come

a long way. While The Great Gatsby ends with

an excited piece of poetry, Tender Is the Night

fades off in the most prosaic rhythms of "his

latest note was post-marked from Hornell, New

York, which is some distance from Geneva and a very small town; in any case he is almost certainly in that section of the country, in one town or another" (p. 315). The holocaust of Gatsby's death was somehow still magnificent, but by _Tender Is the Night_, disillusionment with sentimentalism is complete, and the fall is merciless. We see Dick Diver denied a moving death; instead, he is left to degenerate in the provinces. And somehow Nicole, harder than Daisy and burdened with fewer regrets, has our sympathies. The modern romantic woman, careless and almost mindless of the past, survives in an intensified present.

The night is tender, delicate, and fragrant enough, but it is soon ended. The men can never let it go, and the women always do. It makes them hard, beautiful, and merciless. Fitzgerald knew the dangers of sentimentalism, but still it was impossible for him, and his haunted men, to abandon the debilitating past.

Nicole Diver is perhaps the most favorably treated of Fitzgerald's beautiful and cruel women; we are somehow on her side even after she leaves Dick, and it is significant that we hope Nicole finds someone better than the tan Tommy Barban.

The dilemma is real; either the past plagues or the sense of the advance into the future hardens. There are, however, important characters in Fitzgerald's novels who do seem to find a middle ground. Nick Carraway rejects the carelessness of the rich as they ride their fast cars into the future, leaving shambles behind them, and he rejects the futility of Gatsby's attempt to recreate a dead world. But somehow by abandoning both these references he hangs rather flimsily in the present, a charming but thin-blooded observer. Rosemary Hoyt, in _Tender Is the Night_, is another character who is considerate of both the past and the future. Somehow she remains insignificant. She

doesn't even make a proper exit in the book;
she simply never shows up again after page
289. Practical, thrifty, utterly without
mystery, she is described flatly--Dick "could
possibly have made up Rosemary--he could never
have made up her mother" (p. 165). Theodore
Gross notes her inadequacy when he states that
she is "dominated by her mother and by Hollywood to the degree that she has not yet lived
up to adult standards."[9] "Miss Television,"
Dick calls her, and if she offers a new essence
of a continent, as Nicole is said to have done,
Romantic America is truly gone. As Mr. Gross
suggests, the tragedies of the lives of Gatsby
and Dick Diver are not merely personal, but
represent the decline of the country.[10] When
Nick Carraway says that Long Island's vanished
trees "that had made way for Gatsby's house,
had pandered in whispers to the last and greatest of human dreams" (p. 182), the chill of the
wasteland is on his lips. A new age may be

upon America, neither romantic nor sentimental,
but somehow inadequate, insignificant, and
uninspiring in a difficult modern world.

NOTES

[1]F. Scott Fitzgerald, _This Side of Paradise_ (New York: Scribner's, 1920), p. 177.

[2]Malcolm Cowley, "Fitzgerald: The Double Man," _Saturday Review of Literature_, 24 February 1951, p. 10.

[3]John Keats, _The Poetical Works of John Keats_, ed. H. W. Garrod (London: Oxford Univ. Press, 1956), p. 220.

[4]F. Scott Fitzgerald, _The Great Gatsby_ (New York: Scribner's, 1925), p. 111.

[5]F. Scott Fitzgerald, _The Beautiful and Damned_ (New York: Scribner's, 1922), pp. 166-67.

[6]It is interesting to note that a study of Fitzgerald's women in relation to Keats's poetry shows them extremely close to the lady of "La Belle Dame sans Merci," one of the poems Fitzgerald alludes to most often in his early novels.

[7]F. Scott Fitzgerald, _Tender Is the Night_ (New York: Scribner's, 1933), p. 291.

NOTES (Continued)

[8]*The Art of F. Scott Fitzgerald*, trans. Charles Matz and Sergio Perosa (Ann Arbor: Univ. of Michigan Press, 1965), p. 117.

[9]Theodore L. Gross, "F. Scott Fitzgerald: The Hero in Retrospect," *South Atlantic Quarterly*, 67 (Winter 1964), 72.

[10]Gross, pp. 68-70.

BIBLIOGRAPHY

Cowley, Malcolm. "Fitzgerald: The Double Man."
Saturday Review of Literature, 24 February 1951, pp. 9-10, 42-44.

Fitzgerald, F. Scott. The Beautiful and
Damned. New York: Scribner's, 1922.

_____. The Great Gatsby. New York:
Scribner's, 1924.

_____. Tender Is the Night. New York:
Scribner's, 1933.

_____. This Side of Paradise. New York:
Scribner's, 1920.

Gross, Theodore L. "F. Scott Fitzgerald: The
Hero in Retrospect." South Atlantic
Quarterly, 67 (Winter 1968), 64-77.

Keats, John. The Poetical Works of John Keats,
ed. H. W. Garrod. London: Oxford Univ.
Press, 1956.

Perosa, Sergio. The Art of F. Scott Fitzgerald,
trans. Charles Matz and Sergio Perosa.
Ann Arbor: Univ. of Michigan Press, 1965.

Index of Authors